Simply Proust

Simply Proust

JACK JORDAN

SIMPLY CHARLY
NEW YORK

Copyright © 2020 by Jack Jordan

Cover Illustration by José Ramos
Cover Design by Scarlett Rugers

All rights reserved. No part of this publication may be reproduced, distributed, or transmitted in any form or by any means, including photocopying, recording, or other electronic or mechanical methods, without the prior written permission of the publisher, except in the case of brief quotations embodied in critical reviews and certain other noncommercial uses permitted by copyright law. For permission requests, write to the publisher at the address below.

permissions@simplycharly.com

ISBN: 978-1-943657-20-9

Brought to you by http://simplycharly.com

Contents

	Praise for *Simply Proust*	vii
	Other *Great Lives*	x
	Series Editor's Foreword	xi
	Preface	xii
	À *la recherche du temps perdu* (*In Search of Lost Time*)	xix
1.	Marcel Proust's Early Days	1
2.	Out and About	13
3.	*In Search of Lost Time*	21
4.	Final Years	35
5.	The Narrator: Travels in the Space-Time Continuum	42
6.	A Search for Certainty	51
7.	Transportation	61
8.	Proust and the Human Sciences	75
9.	Proust the Naturalist	84
10.	Three Types of Observation	90
11.	The Reader: Riding the Proust Wave	103
	Sources	111
	Suggested Reading	112
	About the Author	115
	A Word from the Publisher	116

Praise for *Simply Proust*

"*Simply Proust* is an excellent introduction and guide to Proust's fascinating life and his monumental work *In Search of Lost Time*. Themes such as love, jealousy, snobbery, voyeurism, and brothels, as well as characters in Proust's novel, are treated in an engaging, entertaining manner. Jack Jordan's book is a joy to read, full of interesting information, and is highly recommended."
 –**Cynthia Gamble, Honorary Research Fellow, University of Exeter, UK**

"*Simply Proust* pulls off with ease the arduous task of making Marcel Proust's masterwork accessible, sacrificing none of the complexity that makes it one of the most important novels of the 20th Century. To do this, Jack Jordan vividly paints the vast cultural, scientific, and philosophical background that fed *In Search of Lost Time*. Armed with this knowledge, both new and repeat readers are bound to gain fresh insights into the brilliance of Proust's novel."
 –**Hervé G. Picherit, Associate Professor of French, University of Texas at Austin**

"In this fast-paced book, Jack Jordan condenses a lifetime of teaching and research on Proust into a lively and accessible format. Jordan introduces us to Proust, his family, and his friends, all the while taking care to explain and respect Proust's own thoughts on the gap between life and work, between the social self and the hidden, creative self. Jordan inspires us to read, or reread, Proust's novel, inviting us to 'Take those long sentences and paragraphs as a surfer would big waves.' Jordan brings out, in particular, the modernity of Proust's novel: its love of speed, motion, and technology; its engagement with the latest scientific developments in physics, evolution, and psychology."

–Jennifer Rushworth, Associate Professor in French and Comparative Literature, University College London, UK

"Professor Jack Jordan's richly contextualized introduction to Proust revisits the intricate and quasi-mythologized relationship between the writer's life and work in surprisingly lucid ways. From biographical facts through contemporaneous science and sociology to novelistic interpretations, these 11 highly accessible and introspective chapters enthrall the reader to embark on an exciting journey through the Proustian 'space-time continuum.' *Simply Proust* is written with considerable erudition, witticism, and poise, and is also sprinkled with practical tips for a literary amateur's budding Proust pilgrimage."

–Shuangyi Li, Research Fellow in French and Comparative Literature, Centre for Languages and Literature, Lund University, Sweden

"Jack Jordan's *Simply Proust* is a perfect introduction to *In Search of Lost Time*, one of the greatest novels of the 20th century, as well as to its author, Marcel Proust. After an excellent biographical section that connects Proust's life to his work, it presents and analyzes the multiple facets of the novel in a compact and accessible fashion. *Simply Proust* especially emphasizes the French novelist's modern outlook and shows how his view of the world is closely linked to the scientific discoveries of his time. Yet, it also demonstrates how *In Search of Lost Time* is a fascinating voyage of self-discovery for today's reader."

–Pascal Ifri, editor-in-chief of *Bulletin Marcel Proust* & Professor of French, Brown University

"Although simplicity is not usually associated with *In Search of Lost Time*, Professor Jack Jordan does a remarkable job of rendering Marcel Proust's masterpiece accessible. The engaging biography section describes how Proust drew on real-life figures and on his own complex emotions to capture an entire era so vividly that readers feel they have lived there themselves. A thematic section provides a catalog of the perspectives, techniques, and patterns Proust uses to weave the 3000 pages of his seven novels into a brilliant whole capable of changing our views on our own lives. A deeply informed and highly readable introduction."

–Catherine Le Gouis, Professor of French, Mount Holyoke College

"*Simply Proust* provides a wonderfully engaging look not only at the life and work of Marcel Proust, but also at the convoluted relationship that obtains between them. Demonstrating wide-ranging knowledge of Proust's monumental masterpiece, *In Search of Lost Time*, and of the cultural, personal, and social contexts in which it was written, Jack Jordan brings out the astonishing narrative richness, variability–and sheer strangeness–of Proust's work, moving effortlessly between discussions of–among other things–the significance of new technologies (including planes, trains, and automobiles) in the novel, of the relationship between Einstein's theories of relativity and Proust's own investigations in the space-time continuum, of Proust's attempts to describe the workings of the unconscious, and of the relationship between the experience of reading Proust and of hypnotism. Written with enviable clarity and humor, *Simply Proust* is also, on a more light-hearted note, a rich source of funny anecdotes from Proust's life, including details of his addiction to ice cream."

–Thomas Baldwin, Reader in French and co-director of the Centre for Modern European Literature, University of Kent

Other *Great Lives*

Simply Austen by Joan Klingel Ray
Simply Beckett by Katherine Weiss
Simply Beethoven by Leon Plantinga
Simply Chekhov by Carol Apollonio
Simply Chomsky by Raphael Salkie
Simply Chopin by William Smialek
Simply Darwin by Michael Ruse
Simply Descartes by Kurt Smith
Simply Dickens by Paul Schlicke
Simply Dirac by Helge Kragh
Simply Einstein by Jimena Canales
Simply Eliot by Joseph Maddrey
Simply Euler by Robert E. Bradley
Simply Faulkner by Philip Weinstein
Simply Fitzgerald by Kim Moreland
Simply Freud by Stephen Frosh
Simply Gödel by Richard Tieszen
Simply Hegel by Robert L. Wicks
Simply Hitchcock by David Sterritt
Simply Joyce by Margot Norris
Simply Machiavelli by Robert Fredona
Simply Napoleon by J. David Markham & Matthew Zarzeczny
Simply Nietzsche by Peter Kail
Simply Riemann by Jeremy Gray
Simply Sartre by David Detmer
Simply Tolstoy by Donna Tussing Orwin
Simply Stravinsky by Pieter van den Toorn
Simply Turing by Michael Olinick
Simply Wagner by Thomas S. Grey
Simply Wittgenstein by James C. Klagge

Series Editor's Foreword

Simply Charly's "Great Lives" series offers brief but authoritative introductions to the world's most influential people–scientists, artists, writers, economists, and other historical figures whose contributions have had a meaningful and enduring impact on our society.

Each book provides an illuminating look at the works, ideas, personal lives, and the legacies these individuals left behind, also shedding light on the thought processes, specific events, and experiences that led these remarkable people to their groundbreaking discoveries or other achievements. Additionally, every volume explores various challenges they had to face and overcome to make history in their respective fields, as well as the little-known character traits, quirks, strengths, and frailties, myths, and controversies that sometimes surrounded these personalities.

Our authors are prominent scholars and other top experts who have dedicated their careers to exploring each facet of their subjects' work and personal lives.

Unlike many other works that are merely descriptions of the major milestones in a person's life, the "Great Lives" series goes above and beyond the standard format and content. It brings substance, depth, and clarity to the sometimes-complex lives and works of history's most powerful and influential people.

We hope that by exploring this series, readers will not only gain new knowledge and understanding of what drove these geniuses, but also find inspiration for their own lives. Isn't this what a great book is supposed to do?

Charles Carlini, Simply Charly
New York City

Preface

When someone asks if you have read Marcel Proust (1871–1922), the question usually refers to his 3,000-page novel, In Search of Lost Time. Though a prolific writer in numerous genres, without the publication of his masterpiece it is unlikely that his name would have become as well-known as it has. Some individuals who have read In Search of Lost Time consider it to be the greatest novel ever written. Others are more limited in their praise, describing it as the greatest novel of the 20th century or in the French language. Whatever the case may be, it is rare, if not unique to Proust, that a writer had devoted his entire life to creating one novel whose vision reaches from the details of his own life and times to a metaphorical description of the essence of man.

For many, Proust's name is also often synonymous with "difficult to understand." The most obvious reasons for this are the size of the novel and the (in)famous length of some of his sentences. Take those long sentences and paragraphs as a surfer would big waves. Enjoy the ride as long as you can, then have fun falling into what a British academic Malcolm Bowie called the "large tidal movements" that make up "Proust's gritty, breezy, and salty book." Let yourself go and enjoy letting the currents take you where you have not been before.

Since Proust first tried to publish his novel, some readers have had difficulty understanding the lack of an obvious chronological development in characters and plot. Some have found his descriptions of the very ordinary experiences and things that make up daily life to be boring. Swann's Way, the first of the seven volumes that make up In Search of Lost Time, was rejected several times, most famously by André Gide, editor of La Nouvelle Revue Française, the leading French publisher at the time. He later said it was the biggest mistake of his career. Alfred Humblot, the general editor of Ollendorf, Proust's second choice, also rejected it.

"My dear friend," Humblot wrote. "I might be dead from the neck up, but rack my brains as I may, I fail to understand why a man needs thirty pages to describe how he tosses and turns in his bed before falling asleep."

His reaction was not uncommon. But, while seeing what lies on the surface in Proust's novel, he did not perceive what lies below the mundane, ordinary experiences shared by everyone. The times spent falling asleep and waking up are precious parts of the territory that make up the novel's quest. They are the bridges between each person's conscious and unconscious states and can ultimately lead one to the underlying meaning of his novel, which Proust described as a "series of novels of the Unconscious."

Proust finally had to publish *Swann's Way* himself. Despite its slow start, the praise for this innovative novel started pouring in. The numerous translations that are still being done attest to this and the rest of *In Search of Lost Time*'s continuing, universal appeal; properly presented, these aspects are part of what can make the novel more appealing and better understood by modern readers.

Though Proust's novel reflects so well today's modern, relativistic worldview, it is also rich in the particulars of his time. While not an autobiography, this masterpiece is profoundly rooted in his life. He used what he learned from his family, his friends, himself, and the world he lived in and observed with the passion of an artist and the detached perspective of a scientist to create the world of his novel. He enthusiastically embraced, observed, analyzed, and wrote about who and what he experienced—from the smallest details to the most general laws he saw governing man and the world. The end of the 19th century and the beginning of the 20th was a period of great change in science, technology, psychology, and art. Man's relationship to the world around him was being changed by the popular use of trains and the introduction of cars and planes; the increased speed changed his relationship to time and space. Distance was no longer fixed, time and space no longer absolutes.

The arts lie at the heart of Proust's novel, but the sciences provide the tools needed to arrive at the end of the search. Chief among them is psychology. It provided a scientific methodology to reach the essence of "self" and the terminology to express it, taking the search beyond a vague, romanticized notion of man's identity. As this book will show, it also takes the search outside the novel and makes the reader a member of the quest. The results can be exciting and unexpected.

As with Proust's masterpiece, there are aspects to his life that have been associated with his name. They range from his childhood sicknesses, privileged existence, close relationship with his mother and the French pastries called madeleines, to his cork-lined room, inversion of night and day, and a snobbish, sedentary and reclusive existence when he was an adult. Some of these deserve further explanation, and others correction. Both will follow.

In Search of Lost Time is the story of the Narrator's search for a vocation. This also describes a long quest in Proust's own life, which served as a narrative for his novel. Until he found this narrative, his voice, and what would be the essential experience of involuntary memory, Proust (and the Narrator) could not start his novel and did not truly consider himself a writer. Without the experience of the special pleasure brought about by a chance encounter with an object in the world that would ultimately provide the foundation for his "immense edifice of memory," the quest both for a vocation and a vision that would eventually result in this masterpiece was a dilettante's dream.

Though memory lies at the heart of Proust's novel, it is only in small part the sentimental journey backward in time that is suggested by the former English translation of the title, *Remembrance of Things Past*. With the current, more literal title, *In Search of Lost Time*, not only is the essential element of Time introduced, but it is also paired with Lost, suggesting multiple meanings. Taken as "wasted," "lost time" can mean the years the Narrator (and Proust) spent going to the many cultural and social events in Paris that include the periods known as the *fin de siècle* and the *belle époque* and continue until after World War I. Some of these sorties included attending certain salons that permitted him to move about in society and to know aristocrats, writers, musicians, and other important social, political, and artistic individuals. He would then write articles and other small pieces for newspapers describing these people and events. Not only did the time that he was not spending on a serious work of literature concern Proust (and the Narrator), but also the reputation that he got for being a superficial chronicler of Parisian social life around the turn of the century would haunt him even after he started to publish his masterpiece. Anything that took him away from the confines of his room where he could work on his novel was time wasted. As it turned out, these activities gave him the substance for much of his novel and provided the reader with an excellent perspective on Proust's life and times.

"Lost time" can also be understood as the temporal aspect of the extraordinary experience he had with the "special pleasure" that takes one outside the limits of time and space. This interpretation leads one to the heart of the Narrator's (and Proust's) quest: the search for the answer to the fundamental philosophical questions, "who am I?" and "what is the nature of the world?" It is the search for the essence of man, world, how either can be known and how can these discoveries be expressed. The unified worldview that results is the philosophical foundation supporting the rich, complex structure of Proust's novel. The paths that lead to this provide a fascinating look into the creative process and form a large and important part of this book.

This "special pleasure" is born from an experience of involuntary memory. In contrast to voluntary memory, it does not rely on rational efforts to retrieve lost memories. It cannot be forced. Through a chance sensory contact, a past feeling comes alive in the present, taking one out of the normal confines of time and space. Only afterward does intelligence play a role. This is one of the most fundamental of the many oppositions, or dualities, that pervade Proust's novel. Other important oppositions include (but are not limited to): Swann's Way, the Guermantes Way (geographic and social); habit, novelty; light, dark; night, day; clear, obscure;

inward, outward; particular, general; micro, macro; enclosed, open; and tragic, comic. All will be shown to be either a synthesis or at least two essential sides of life and the world. Proust also arrived at the two essential parts of any knowledge: a subject to know and an object to be known. This simple opposition or duality (subject-object) lies at the heart of Proust's philosophy and worldview.

The goal of *Simply Proust* is to introduce Proust's unusual life and times and explore the thoughts that inspired him to create his novel. This book also intends to help understand the basic, symmetrical structure, as well as the simple elegance of this seemingly complex novel, and to provide a personal experience for the reader. While we can't go into every particular detail that makes up Proust's edifice, we can see certain patterns that develop from the smallest detail to the structure of the entire novel.

We will look at some of the most important of the Narrator's experiences to see what patterns emerge within the repetitions and changes. These meaningful experiential dots will be connected at the end of the novel using the will, the tools of reason, and intelligence to deduce the essence of man and world, as well as the laws that govern them. By underlining whatever makes an impression, whether understood at the time, the reader may also create dots that, after being looked at from a later perspective, can also create a picture or mosaic that is unique and personal yet rooted in the novel. If a phrase or an idea keeps repeating in your mind, pay attention to it. If you would like to have a colorful perspective of the first few pages of the novel, mark each reference to light in one color and those to time in another. There will be lots of color reflected by these two essential aspects of Proust's entire novel.

The layout of the chapters reflects the two essential relationships to the novel (Author-Novel-Reader). The chapter titled, "Marcel Proust's Early Days," delves into his life and its relationship to *In Search of Lost Time*. His family, friends, and other sources are presented, along with other sources for the events, places, and ideas that occur in the novel.

Due to the important role the Narrator has regarding the author, the novel, and the reader, the discussion of the novel is divided into two parts: "The Narrator: Travels in the Space-Time Continuum" and "A Search for Certainty." The ever-present question of identity continues to play a predominant role in the former. Is there one or several Narrators? Is there one core Self or several selves? What should he be called? How does the Narrator welcome the reader, including him or her in the quest? Through the Narrator's experience of involuntary memory, a causal, positivistic universe is replaced by one based on a synchronistic, acausal worldview where the relationship between time, space, and identity are recreated. In "A Search for Certainty," the major themes and features of the novel are presented in a way that reflects that of *In Search of Lost Time*. It is inductive, moving from the particular to the general, and it moves outward, from the bedroom to the stairs to the house itself. At the end of "Combray," the first part of Swann's Way, the "raised finger of the day" points the way out of the confines of the Narrator's bedroom that will ultimately lead to the certainty that was lost in the darkness of the opening pages of the novel.

Another chapter looks at the essential role the reader plays in the Narrator's quest, how he or she is included, what is the role of the unconscious, and what relevance this can have in one's own life. Proust's (and the Narrator's) experiences with psychology are continued from the previous chapter with an emphasis on the possible role hypnosis plays and how this can affect the reader's experience.

Proust blurs the boundaries that separate the world of the novel from that of the author and from that of the reader. Despite his clear and often-stated opposition to looking at a piece of art (literary, pictorial, etc.) from the side of its creator and his emphasis on the importance of the relationship on the other side of the novel, from that of the reader, the boundary between Proust and the novel is also blurred. One of the means by which this is achieved is by using real historical figures and events alongside fictional characters. This particular mixture is one reason for the historical richness of Proust's novel.

The novel is not short, which in itself limits its general appeal. However, just as it takes time to create a world, it takes time for a person to be transported into it. Ideally, it should be read at night, undisturbed by anyone or anything that might interfere with becoming part of the novel, like the Narrator who, on the first page, describes himself as falling asleep while reading, seemingly becoming the subject of the book. If you do not have the time to read the novel from beginning to end, try reading the first and last volumes together. Try not to let the novel's reputation as being difficult bother you. Just read it and try to hang on because if you give it a chance, you may be in for a ride as rewarding as those taken by Aladdin on his magic carpet in *The Arabian Nights*.

Jack L. Jordan
Orange Beach, Alabama

À la recherche du temps perdu (*In Search of Lost Time*)

1913 Volume I: Du côté de chez Swann (Swann's Way)
1918 Volume II: A l'ombre des jeunes filles en fleurs (Within a Budding Grove)
1920 Volume III: Le Côté de Guermantes (The Guermantes' Way)
1921 Volume IV: Sodome et Gomorrhe (Sodom and Gomorrah)
1923 Volume V: La Prisonnière (The Captive)
1924 Volume VI: Albertine disparue (The Fugitive)
1927 Volume VII: Le Temps retrouvé (Time Regained)

The dates are those of the French versions. For the purpose of simplification, the volumes are summarized under their current titles.

1. Marcel Proust's Early Days

Marcel Valentin Louis Eugène Georges Proust was born on July 10, 1871, in Auteuil, a suburb of Paris. His father, Adrien Proust, was born in 1834 in Illiers, a small town near Chartres, not far from Paris. His mother, Jeanne Clémence Weil, was born in 1849, in Paris. Both of his parents were from relatively wealthy families. His father was Catholic and his mother was Jewish, and even though Marcel and his brother Robert were raised Catholic, religion was not a dominant force in the family. When his parents were married, the Second Empire was ending, and the Third Republic was beginning. It was the start of new Constitutional Laws, establishing a regime based on parliamentary supremacy.

Even for the relatively wealthy, this was not an easy time, and the newlyweds had to survive the sieges and bombardments of the Prussians and then the insurrection of the Communards. The childhood sicknesses that plagued Marcel could be attributed to these circumstances. Later, when he was nine, he almost died from an asthma attack, the first of many to follow and which would have a profound effect on him for the rest of his life. One bright aspect of this illness was that he spent holidays at the beach in Normandy, where he could breathe easier thanks to the sea air. The time he spent there was good for his health, and the area would become a regular vacation destination. The town of Cabourg would become Proust's inspiration for Balbec, the seaside resort featured in his book. His brother, Robert, who was born in 1873, did not suffer from Marcel's ailments and became a doctor, like their father. Though they seem to have gotten along relatively well despite their differences and usual sibling rivalries, Proust's Narrator does not have a brother.

Marcel and his mother were extremely close, and she obviously played the most important role in his life. Both she and her mother, Adèle Weil, were well educated and helped create and nourish his love for literature, art, theater, and music. His grandmother frequented a salon held by Amélie Crémieux, a talented relative and the wife of an important left-wing politician. She met many writers, artists, composers, and politicians there, passing on to her son not only many interesting stories but also a particular and personal relationship with these great artists—a talent that Proust exhibited in the unique and personal experience many individuals have when reading his novel. Along with her appreciation for other 17th-century writers, such as Corneille and Racine, she passed on to her son her love for a French aristocrat, Mme de Sévigné, whose letters to her daughter serve as an example of the devotion that is possible between a parent and a child, and as a chronicle of the court of Louis XIV. Mme de Sévigné is referred to often in the novel and is associated with the Narrator's grandmother. These writings familiarized the future novelist with the value of someone observing and describing the people and events that make up one's life and times. The particular analysis and the presentation, however, belong to the novelist alone.

Marcel spent most of his life in Paris. In 1872, Proust's family moved to the Boulevard Malesherbes, in the 8th arrondissement. He would live in this part of the city for the greater part of his life. The family often stayed at his maternal grandfather's Louis Weil's home in the Auteuil neighborhood. Louis also owned property on boulevard Haussmann, where Proust would later live for 13 years and make famous in *In Search of Lost Time*. There he would eventually install a noise-proof cork-lined bedroom. He would also stay at his aunt Elisabeth's house in Illiers-Combray in north-central France, which Proust immortalized in his novel as Aunt Léonie's house. The fictional house of his uncle Adolphe, meanwhile, will become forbidden territory in the novel, where the young Narrator meets one of his fictional uncle Adolphe's "lady friends," Odette de Crécy, for the first time. In a typically Proustian way, only later will the Narrator and the reader realize that this apparently unimportant, chance encounter is the beginning of something significant and that she is an integral part of the novel. In an equally subtle and apparently inconsequential way, the theme of uncertainty regarding social and sexual identity continues. The inspiration for Odette came principally from a courtesan, Laure Hayman; a photograph of the American singer Marie van Zandt dressed as a man that belonged to his father possibly served as an inspiration for the picture of the young Narrator. Laure and Marcel would become lifelong friends, with Laure referring to the young Marcel as her "little psychologist in porcelain." (The passionate obsession Swann will have for Odette will foreshadow the Narrator's own jealous attempts to realize his love for Albertine and, as the novel travels through the life and times of the Narrator, Odette will also show the impermanence of social hierarchies and be part of the unification of the two "Ways," introduced at the beginning of the novel.)

The houses in Auteuil and Illiers contributed to the creation of the fictional Combray, where the Narrator and his family spent holidays with his Aunt Léonie and her maid, Françoise. However, the majority of events occurred in Illiers, including the tasting of the madeleine pastry and herbal tea. In an interesting reversal of the usual influence the real world may have had on the world of the novel, the town's name is now officially Illiers-Combray. It is from this house that the famous distinction between the two "Ways" are found. For walks, the Narrator's family could take the "Méséglise," "Swann's" Way, or the "Guermantes" Way. Swann's Way was the shorter of the two and the path most often taken. On one of his walks, the Narrator first sees Charles and Odette Swann's daughter, Gilberte, the Narrator's first love. The "Guermantes Way" takes the Narrator and his family along the Vivonne, a river that follows the walk and where he describes the water-lilies that he sees. Impressionist painter Claude Monet created them with paint, and Proust painted them with words. The former "Way" is associated with the bourgeois Swann, and the latter with the aristocratic Guermantes family. The two ways will eventually converge when Gilberte Swann marries Robert de Saint-Loup, a member of the Guermantes family. It will also be united when, with the use of an automobile, both sides could be visited in one day. Though Proust (and the Narrator) was known for his sedentary, enclosed, and sterile existence in Paris, these walks (along with visits to Auteuil) helped create a love for nature and much of his appreciation of it, especially for his beloved hawthorn trees. The house in Illiers-Combray still is one of the more popular Proustian "pilgrimages" to make.

Marcel's mother certainly played the dominant role in Proust's life, but his father's influence and the contacts he made in his extremely successful career as a doctor of epidemiology and other related fields (including psychology) provided many of the sources for the knowledge that went into his novel. Not only did his scientific background influence the young novelist's worldview, but his work both at home and internationally also put him in touch with politicians and diplomats, some of whom made it into the novel as inspirations for characters or are cited with their real names. Both parents were important not only in the creation of the Narrator's family, but also in the two supposedly contradictory worldviews that make up his novel itself.

From 1882 to 1889, Marcel attended what was known for his first year as the Lycée Fontanes and subsequently as the Lycée Condorcet. Records from 1885 show that he was frequently absent due to illness. He made many lifelong friends there and showed an interest in the natural sciences, in particular botany, due at least in part to his excellent and extremely funny teacher, Georges Colomb. These scientific perspectives (and humor) are evident throughout the novel and dominate the beginning of *Sodom and Gomorrah*. In 1888, the greatest influence on Proust was his philosophy professor, Alphonse Darlu (perhaps an inspiration for the writer Bergotte in the novel). He taught Proust a paradoxical mindset, showing him the importance of scientific discovery and the lack of a fixed reality in the world of the senses, which had become two fundamental aspects of Proust's worldview. Darlu's method of teaching can also be seen in Proust's novel, as he taught philosophy in a humorous, often metaphorical way that appealed to Marcel as well as many other students. The traits from these two teachers are inherent to the process by which his philosophical worldview is presented.

The Champs-Elysées neighborhood, where the famous eponymous avenue is located, was Marcel's playground, and he played there often with old and new friends. One day he met Marie de Benardaky there and became infatuated with her. His preoccupation with Marie did not preclude, however, his love for and pursuit of certain male classmates. In November of 1887, he and some of his talented school friends started a literary review called *Le Lundi*. It only survived five months, and afterward Marcel wrote some pieces for *La Revue Lilas*, also produced by Proust and his friends.

The *salon* life

During his last year at Condorcet, his friends were playing another role, providing the *open sesame*—free access—to some of the salons in Paris. It did not hurt that he was young and well-mannered or knew how to flatter, converse, and be generous in sending beautiful bouquets of flowers to the hostess. The salon held by Geneviève Straus was elegant and successful, attended by many aristocrats and famous artists. She was the mother of one of Marcel's school friends, Jacques Bizet (his mother remarried Emile Straus after her husband's death). Soon after marrying, Emile and Geneviève moved to 134 boulevard Haussmann, only a few doors down from where Proust would live years later. Emile was the owner of a wonderful collection of works by contemporary painters, including Claude Monet and Gustave Moreau. Thanks to this combination of connections and talent, he was granted entry into what was for him at that point in his life an unknown, wonderful, and exciting world. Though those attending included such celebrities as the composer Gabriel Fauré, author Guy de Maupassant, painter Edgar Degas, Princess Mathilde (daughter of King Jerome of Westphalia and niece of Napoléon I), and actress Sarah Bernhardt (who appears in Proust's novel both by name and as a possible inspiration for the fictional actress La Berma), Proust was most impressed by an erudite Parisian Charles Haas. Young Marcel admired his manners, style, and social standing. He was the only Jewish member of the elite Jockey Club in Paris and moved in the highest circles. Most importantly, the character of Charles Swann was based at least in part on Charles Haas. From 1889 to 1890, Proust served in the military in Orléans, a city not far from Paris. His less-than-illustrious military career began with his being allowed to live in private quarters in town rather than in the barracks because his constant coughing during the night kept the other soldiers awake. While there, he met men from all social classes. Marcel found something to like in soldiers from all levels of society. His superior officer, Comte Armand-Pierre de Cholet, was not only an aristocrat, but he was also a handsome, 26-year-old bachelor who befriended the 18-year-old cadet. His influence on Proust is apparent in one of his earlier writings and ultimately he would be part of the inspiration for the character Robert de Saint-Loup in *In Search of Lost Time*, a kind and caring Guermantes who looked after the Narrator in many ways, including jumping over people and tables in a restaurant to come to his aid. Proust apparently enjoyed his time in the military so much that he tried to reenlist. His offer was declined.

Marcel's parents were concerned about finding a career for their son, whose main preoccupations were society and literature. At their insistence, he enrolled in university courses. From 1890 to 1895, Proust studied law and political science at the Sorbonne, receiving degrees in both. However, neither field stuck as a career path. During this time, he got to meet Oscar Wilde when the Irish playwright visited Paris. He went to the theater, co-founded a literary review, *Le Banquet*, in which he published 15 short pieces, and went to even more salons than before.

At Princess Mathilde's salon, he met Charles Ephrussi, an art critic who admired Johannes Vermeer. The Dutch master's paintings inspired Proust until (almost quite literally) his death. His favorite painting was Vermeer's *View of Delft*. Ephrussi was impressed with Marcel's knowledge of, and interest in, painting and offered to let him see his collection which, like that at the home of Emile Straus, included paintings by Monet and Moreau. Ephrussi is another real-life figure who inspired the creation of Charles Swann.

In 1892, Proust posed for his portrait with Jacques-Emile Blanche. This painting now hangs in the Musée d'Orsay. Proust kept this portrait in his bedroom. Not long thereafter, he was able to penetrate yet another circle of prominent people from the arts, politics, and still more aristocrats. Madeleine Lemaire's salon would prove to be a treasure trove of individuals from whom Proust would mine characters, and of whom he would make some of his most acerbic observations. It was a microcosm, a world within which he could observe the human species with the "satisfaction of a zoologist."

The number of individuals who attended Lemaire's salon is too large to list here, but some stand out because of their importance to Proust's life and his novel. The hostess would become Proust's friend and provide illustrations for one of his first independently published works, *Pleasure and Days*. Among the musicians Proust might have heard were Camille Saint-Saëns and Gabriel Fauré. He also met Comte Boniface de Castellane ("Boni") who, among other things, would give one of the most lavish parties of the *Belle Epoque*.

In 1893, Lemaire introduced Proust to Comte Robert de Montesquiou-Fezensac. He was elegant, intelligent, and creative. On the other hand, he was also an aristocratic snob who represented French decadence in a sometimes not-so-subtle way. He and Proust would be off-and-on friends for many years but, with de Montesquiou's temperament and demanding ways, and Proust's sometimes reclusive nature, there would be long, haughty silences. Italian painter Giovanni Boldini portrayed him in his refined elegance, holding a cane (that would draw some jokes, carrying a sexual innuendo among certain individuals) in *Count Robert de Montesquiou* (1897). Like most characters in *In Search of Lost Time*,

Charlus is a creation based on a combination of several individuals in Proust's world, but the relatively direct affinity between de Montesquiou and the Baron de Charlus in Proust's novel is often made more obvious than with many of the real people who served as the inspiration for his other characters. In one example, Proust described Charlus and the stylish, deliberate simplicity of his evening coat with a touch of red in a ribbon and a medal showing his membership as a Knight of the religious Order of Malta. This reminds the Narrator of American painter James Whistler's *Harmony in Black and White* but he comments that it should be *Harmony in Black, White, and Red* because of the ribbon holding the Maltese Cross, which is made up of white, black, and red enamel. It was not this sort of parallel that enraged Montesquiou. Rather, it was being the principal inspiration for one of literature's most decadent homosexuals. As strange a character as he may seem, his love is no different than Swann's or the Narrator's. Love hurts everyone, not only a masochist like Charlus. Each character is to blame for the impossible personal situation that love has created; Swann with Odette, the Narrator with Albertine, and Charlus with Morel–a young musician he has "adopted" and helped introduce to society. Despite his protests that there was no relationship and Charlus was a fictional character, Proust's explanation did not fool Montesquiou and this did nothing to help an already stormy friendship. In fact, his inspiration also came from the Baron Doäzan, who he met at a salon held by another hostess. Whistler was also an inspiration for part of the character of Elstir, the painter in the novel.

    Most importantly for *In Search of Lost Time*, Lemaire's bourgeois salon, her "clan" of the faithful, her horror of "bores" and viciousness toward "deserters" who attended events other than hers, as well as certain mannerisms (for instance, the way she laughed), all made it into the novel in the form of the salon of Mme Verdurin. Many memorable events occur there–such as the concerts of the music of the fictional composer Vinteuil–but the social chemistry is often stirred and her salon results in some of the more comic–and tragic–scenes in the novel. Her salon shows many of the turns of the social kaleidoscope, in itself representing the rise of the influence of the bourgeoisie and the decline of that of the aristocracy.

In 1894, Proust met a young composer, singer, and pianist named Reynaldo Hahn at Lemaire's salon. Marcel was 22 and Reynaldo only 19, but they had more in common than just their Jewish-Catholic backgrounds, and they became close friends. Later, at Lemaire's home at Réveillon, Marcel and Reynaldo were taking a walk in her garden when Marcel stopped to look at some Bengal roses. According to Hahn, this was the first of many episodes when Marcel appeared to be in a trance, in total communication with nature or art where "his superhuman intelligence and sensitivity ... reached the root of things and discovered what no one else could see." When Proust put the Narrator in a similar situation with his beloved hawthorn trees, we see that much more was happening. He was not only looking outward, toward the essence of things, but also inward, toward the essence of his own nature.

Characters rooted in real life

In mid-September of that year, Marcel joined his mother at Trouville, on the Normandy coast. Later that month, he asked Hahn to join him, even though the season was ending and the hotel would soon be closing. Proust often stayed as long as he could. The quiet periods at the end of the season (and sometimes afterwards) allowed him to get to know the people who worked there. He had a close rapport with the staff, genuinely caring about them, showing a real interest in their families, their dialects, their histories, and their gossip. And he was a generous tipper. Simply because they are not famous or unnamed in the novel does not mean that they were not a source of inspiration for much that appears in the book, at the Grand Hotel in Balbec or elsewhere. In Paris, waiters from the Ritz Hotel served a similar role, as did those who worked in his home.

In *In Search of Lost Time*, Charlus will show the possibility of an additional sexual component by his interest in and attraction to the young men who ran the streetcars.

Proust returned to Paris by the end of September. He wrote several stories that introduced some of the basic elements later found in his novel, including the goodnight kiss from the Narrator's mother, jealousy, and the need to possess the other, something that does not end well for the Narrator, for Swann, or for Charlus. In these earlier pieces, written when he was 23, one can also see Proust's search for both physiological and psychological laws that would explain human behavior. During the same period, he forgot to register for his exam in an advanced degree in philosophy. His parents' concerns could only be growing.

In December of 1894, a French army officer, Captain Alfred Dreyfus, was convicted of treason for allegedly sharing military secrets with the Germans. He was summarily judged and sent to Devil's Island, a French penal colony off the coast of French Guiana in South America. Evidence was subsequently found that showed he was innocent. The country was (and to a certain extent still is) divided between Dreyfusards and anti-Dreyfusards, socialists and conservatives. Anti-Dreyfusards were generally French nationalists who saw conspiracies against France and its military establishment and blamed the Jews. It was even argued that, because of their religion, Jews could not be considered to be French. In 1898, writer Emile Zola published his famous letter "J'accuse" in support of Dreyfus. This resulted in the court's decision to put the famous writer on trial. A staunch Dreyfusard, Proust regularly attended the trial in support of Zola and started a "Petition of the Intellectuals." He was able to get signatures from many prominent individuals. This cannot have been an easy time for Proust's father, who was an anti-Dreyfusard. A socialite with no job prospects and now a socialist, Marcel was showing few of the practical values his parents had been trying to instill since he was a child.

In the novel, it is Mme Verdurin who attends Zola's court appearances, and her salon reflects her Dreyfusard sentiments.

Proust made a parallel between Jews and homosexuals, calling both "cursed races." The French imprisoned Dreyfus and the English imprisoned Oscar Wilde, but homosexuals were being mistreated and even jailed on both sides of the channel. The conservatives (though not excluded from homosexual practices themselves) suspected both. In the last volume of the novel, *Time Regained*, the Narrator sees a suspicious character furtively entering a building during World War I. He suspects that it is a spy, but finds out it is a homosexual, uneasy about being seen entering Jupien's male brothel. Charlus is suspected of being a spy when he offers a relatively large sum of money to a boy who is relieved when he realizes that it is only his body he is being asked to give up and not his country.

Health woes

In the middle of 1895, Proust was given a minor job in the Mazarine Library. He showed up once before starting to take sick leave, which lasted for months. He took several trips, one with his mother to Kreuznach, a well-known health spa in Germany, where he began *Jean Santeuil*, an intended novel that, though it held seeds of what would become *In Search of Lost Time*, lacked the structure, depth, narrative, and the vision that would make *In Search of Lost Time* his masterpiece. One of the most fruitful of these seeds was the extra-temporal experience that comes from a memory associated with a sense contact with an object in the physical world. When his fifth year of sick leave ended, it was not extended.

Proust's father, a doctor, did research in a number of areas. One was neurasthenia, the 19th-century term for what today is called chronic fatigue syndrome. He and a colleague wrote a book, *How to live with Neurasthenia*. The symptoms fit his son perfectly. It was directed particularly toward members of the upper classes, who spent their time going out and living excessively by eating and drinking too much and for too long and having strange sleeping habits. The list of symptoms includes insomnia, hypochondria, asthma, fear of drafts, auditory hypersensitivity, abulia (the loss of willpower), and a lot of masturbating. Perhaps Dr. Proust was thinking of his son as he co-wrote the book. Most of these symptoms are part of what made Marcel who he was and were part of, if not dictated by, what finally led to the creation of his masterpiece. Of all the problems, the lack of willpower perhaps concerned Proust the most because, as his Narrator states, it is the "greatest of all vices." Nothing will get done without it. *In Search of Lost Time* is evidence that he could eventually deal with this symptom. But Proust's (and the Narrator's) quest requires much more. He would also need the ability to put aside his will and the dictates of conscious reason for a passive state, receptive not only to the book growing in him, but also to chance encounters in the external world and an instinct, a vision that belongs to the world of art. Proust's gymnastic swings between two such opposed states, the voluntary and the involuntary, could not have been easy.

2. Out and About

In 1896, Proust self-published *Pleasures and Days*, a collection of short pieces with illustrations by Lemaire. In the same year, his uncle Louis died. Proust's mother inherited half the estate and he would eventually move into the home at 102 boulevard Haussmann that was part of the inheritance 10 years later. Marcel's health problems (real or imagined) continued and, combined with his difficulties sleeping at night, he was taking drugs containing narcotics. He became depressed and even more extravagant in his spending, especially for someone with no income. His parents' concerns were mounting.

In February of 1897, a columnist named Jean Lorrain wrote a scathing and homophobic article about *Pleasures and Days*. He said it was filled with "inane flirtations in a dated, pretentious" affair with Lucien Daudet. No matter that the columnist was also a homosexual, Proust did not take this well.

Proust may have had many physical ailments and peculiar habits, but in spirit, he was strong, according to Paul Morand, a writer, diplomat, and friend of Proust in his later years. Morand wrote that "Proust had a lot of authority, what the English call 'poise,' ... and, at the same time, lots of courage. He looked at you right in the eye, with a somewhat defiant air, like d'Artagnan [the character from Alexandre Dumas' *The Three Musketeers*], head back. He was very courageous." He also had a temper and, when his honor was questioned, he could react "with extreme prejudice." Proust challenged Lorrain to a duel. Both shots missed their target, and the duel was over.

Despite all this, he continued working on *Jean Santeuil*. But it was to be an unfinished novel, and Proust wanted not only to be a writer, but also a novelist. He did not want to write in the emotional, Romantic tradition. His tough-mindedness is reflected in his Narrator's "x-raying" individuals, penetrating the barriers of social dissimulation to arrive at the essence of the human species, and in his desire to write like the French realists Honoré de Balzac, Gustave Flaubert, and Stendhal. If there were to be any Romantic aspects, they would lie in the focus on the Self. However, unlike the Romantics, Proust used the methodology and terminology of the newly emerging science of psychology and focused his penetrating vision on the Self and the sensorial, involuntary type of memory that lies at the heart of his quest. On the other hand, like the realists, he included the social and political events of his time, adding real-world pillars to the "immense edifice of memory" that is In Search of Lost Time.

In 1898, Proust traveled to Amsterdam and stayed at the Amstel Hotel to see an exhibition of 125 paintings by Rembrandt. Art, like music and theater, was always something that kept Proust in motion, going out, and traveling to have firsthand experience with the original works.

Rembrandt's use of clear sources of light, so different from the diffuse, dappled effects of the Impressionists, was "in some way the very light of his thoughts." Both sorts of lighting are found throughout In Search of Lost Time.

Inspired by travel

The year 1899 marked the "*fin de siècle*"–the end of the 19th century. In the early fall of that year, Proust traveled to Evian-les-Bains and stayed at the Splendide Hotel. The original idea for the restaurant at the Grand Hotel in Balbec to be described as an aquarium comes from his time at the restaurant at the Splendide Hotel. With its revolutionary use of iron and glass, the hotel represented the newest and most modern in architecture and was an essential part of the style known as *art nouveau* (new art). Developments around 1900, including the World's Fair held in Paris, were all signs of modernism.

The first evidence of Proust riding in an automobile also happened in 1899. He traveled from Evian to Geneva, Switzerland by train, and was picked up at the station in a motorcar owned by the Prince de Chimay. The two drove to the nearby Château of Coppet (former home to Mme de Staël and currently owned by her great-grandson, the Comte d'Haussonville). The beautiful drive, combined with the speed of the automobile, impressed Proust.

By this time, the writer was close to becoming a novelist. *Jean Santeuil* may not have been a success, but it contained much of what Proust would later use in *In Search of Lost Time*. The autobiographical details, some characters, and episodes, as well as looking at the whole process involved in creating a work of art that also means a quest of the nature of one's Self are there. His failure at making *Jean Santeuil* into a finished novel would itself be used. It would become a motivating force for the Narrator and the central storyline of Proust's masterpiece: the search for a vocation as a great novelist. His father must have been thrilled when Marcel told him, "I still believe that anything I do outside of literature and philosophy will be just so much time wasted."

The year 1900 brought changes, many of them increasing the speed of everyday life. Proust embraced all things modern in science, technology, and the arts, including them in his novel. Before we look too far forward, however, the death in January 1900 of John Ruskin, a prominent British art critic, made Proust look backward to the medieval architecture Ruskin described. Proust had already been working on essays pertaining to Ruskin and wrote an obituary for the newspaper *Le Figaro*. Ruskin's aesthetics, especially the cathedrals he described, made a strong impression on Proust and made their way into his novel. For several years (with a lot of help from his mother), Marcel devoted himself to translating and annotating Ruskin's texts. In 1904, he published *La Bible d'Amiens* and in 1906 he released his second complete translation from the original English (*Sesame and the Lilies*) into French (*Sésame et les lys*).

The first years of the 20th century were eventful for Proust, in good ways and bad. After almost three decades of living at the Boulevard Malesherbes, the Prousts moved to the rue de Courcelles in 1900. Marcel took two trips to Venice that year. Shortly after, he became infatuated with the diplomat Bertrand de Fénelon who, with his good looks and bisexuality, became part of the inspiration for the character Robert de Saint-Loup. In 1902, Proust and Fénelon traveled to Bruges in Belgium to see an exhibition of Flemish art. Later, they met in Amsterdam and stayed at the Hôtel de l'Europe. Before joining Fénelon in The Hague, Proust took a short trip to Haarlem to see the Frans Hals paintings that are still housed in a former orphanage. In The Hague, they went to the Mauritshuis Royal Art Gallery, where Marcel saw Vermeer's *View of Delft*. Several of the few paintings by Vermeer still hang there.

On Thursday, November 26, 1903, Adrien Proust died after suffering a stroke two days earlier. Proust would use part of this experience in his description of a son at his father's funeral. Adrien was buried in the Père Lachaise Cemetery in Paris, as his wife and Marcel would be in their time. The Proust family gravesite is worth visiting. Notes left by admirers quietly attest to the profound effect the writer still has on many individuals. After the deaths of his father and uncle Louis, Marcel had approximately $850,000 in today's money. He had few living expenses as he still lived at home with his mother. His mother kept control of the money and Marcel was kept on a relatively short financial leash.

Shortly after publishing *La Bible d'Amiens* at the beginning of 1904, the French novelist Maurice Barrès asked Proust to translate works of another author. Proust declined, explaining that he still had some translations of Ruskin's writings to do "and after that I shall try to translate my own poor soul, if it doesn't die in the meantime." The French philosopher Henri Bergson wrote Proust to thank him for sending him a copy of *La Bible d'Amiens*. In April of the same year, Proust wrote to a friend, Marie Nordlinger, that he missed her visit because of all the pollen aggravating his asthma. Since he could not go out and see flowers in bloom, she went to a Japanese import store and bought him some packets containing dried paper pellets that expanded into flowers, houses, and tiny people when you added water. This would make it into his novel, the early part of his novel. It concluded the first section in an expansive, crescendo-like fashion, reinforcing the experience of the madeleine cake by drawing a clear parallel between the two.

On June 7, Proust got up before the afternoon in order to visit a collection of 39 paintings by Monet. Vermeer, Monet, and Rembrandt stand out among the many artists mentioned in Proust's novel, and, more subtly, the paintings hanging in the novel help illuminate his world.

Another way Proust reconciled his nocturnal existence with the need to adapt to a daytime activity was by not going to bed. He stayed up on June 24, 1905, in order to see a collection of Whistler's paintings. He drank his usual strong, hot coffee and went to bed after seeing the paintings. Once again, art (and music) had the force of attraction to draw Proust out of the tight orbit of his home.

On Tuesday, September 26, 1905, Proust's mother died. Three weeks earlier, she and Marcel had returned to the Hôtel Splendide in Evian when Jeanne fell ill from a kidney ailment and could not walk without help. She wanted to have a picture taken but was afraid she would not photograph well. Marcel's last image of her would show her debilitated state. This too would make it into his novel in one of its most poignant moments. While at Balbec with his grandmother, the Narrator describes a similar scene when she debates whether to have her picture taken. The Narrator is far from omniscient and is submerged in the action. He also included how he saw his mother, rejuvenated in death, as a description of the Narrator's grandmother after she died.

Proust was devastated and sought medical treatment. Looking for the best clinic in Paris, he asked a friend, Anna de Noailles, to see if her husband had a suggestion. Anna had suffered from depression in 1901 and spent three months at Dr. Paul Sollier's clinic. Earlier that year, on July 28, Proust had gone to see Dr. Edouard Brissaud, who referred him to Dr. Sollier for treatment, as he had done in Anna's case. It was then that Proust declared he was "going to write a book about doctors." He evidently tried to make it to the clinic, but never felt well enough to go. After his mother's death, he was able to get Dr. Sollier to make a house call. When the doctor came to Proust's home, he talked him into leaving immediately for his clinic at Boulogne-sur-Seine, on the outskirts of Paris. Proust was not impressed with psychology, preferring the traditional type of doctor who, like the one sculpted at the Reims Cathedral, examines a bottle of urine. He spent the rest of the fall there and left near the end of January 1906.

A busy life

Marcel and his brother received one-half of the inheritance each. His part of the estate included a quarter share of the house at 102 boulevard Haussmann, in addition to money. In total, Proust was a millionaire approximately worth $4.6 million in today's money. Without the financial controls from his mother, he was free to spend it. And he did. He gambled and lost a considerable sum on the stock market.

At the end of September 1906, Proust moved from his home on the rue de Courcelles to the house he inherited on boulevard Haussmann. The former was too large and expensive, and it was where both of his parents had died. Proust decided to move for sentimental reasons, even though boulevard Haussmann was among the noisiest and dustiest places in the city. It was not an easy transition for Proust. After he had finally moved, he had to deal with renovations in other apartments in his new surroundings. He tried using his social and political connections to stop the noise. When that did not work, he paid some workers at one of the other apartments to work at night instead of during the day so he could get some sleep in the morning. All the noise and dust from the street and the construction aggravated his asthma and sleep disorder to the point that he was using more drugs than usual to help him sleep, with lots of coffee to help him wake up.

In March 1907, Proust published an article in the newspaper *Le Figaro*, titled "On Reading" ("*Sur la lecture*"). Some important parts of what would become *In Search of Lost Time* can be found in the article, including the "outrageous priestesses of the Invisible, the Young Ladies of the Telephone." Marcel's close friendship with Reynaldo Hahn continued, and he was invited to hear Reynaldo perform two of his compositions at a musical event held at the Princesse de Polignac's home. While listening to the music, Proust was looking around, noticing how old some of the friends he had not seen in years had become. His description of the ravages time can bring in our transitory existence made it into the last volume of the novel in a darkly funny ball held at the home of the Princesse de Guermantes. In the meantime, unsettling novelty had given way to familiar and comforting habit, and Proust would spend the next seven summers vacationing at the Grand-Hôtel in Cabourg. He would write part of his novel there and included it as one of the Narrator's three main locales in *In Search of Lost Time*. It is a great Proustian pilgrimage. You can stay in the room where Proust slept. The hotel has used the beautiful leather-bound books of the Pléiade to fill the bookshelves whose glass fronts reflect the view out the dormer window described in the novel. Among the Pléiades, there are some of Proust's contemporaries (Colette) and some of his favorite authors, including Charles Baudelaire and Gérard de Nerval. You can still ride the little elevator down to eat in the restaurant and look out of your "aquarium" onto the people on the Promenade, as well as the sand, sea, and sky beyond.

Proust had several friends who rented villas in the area. In order to see them and the region's architecture, he managed to get up and out in the daytime with, at a minimum, lots of hot, strong coffee. In Paris, his usual day began at around 10 a.m. He would be ready to do something around 4 p.m. In order to get to his wide-ranging attractions, Proust hired automobiles. This truly made the trip as important as the destination, and both would also make it into his novel. Proust used motorcars and drivers from one of the first car rental agencies in Paris, *Taxi-mètres Unic*. The director of the agency was Jacques Bizet, an old friend of Proust. It was through him that Proust met two drivers, Odilon Albaret and Alfred Agostinelli. Along with his experiences riding in automobiles, these two individuals would play important roles in his life and, directly or indirectly, in his novel. From 1914 to 1922, his most productive years in writing *In Search of Lost Time*, Odilon's wife, Céleste Albaret was instrumental both in facilitating the writing process and in helping Proust with all of his demanding and unusual habits necessary for him to survive and create. Céleste's book, *Monsieur Proust*, written years later when she was 82, is a personal and touching perspective on Proust, the man and his creative process. Agostinelli would take a greater role in Proust's life and serve as one of the models for Albertine, one of the novel's most important characters. These individuals, as well as the experiences they provided, will be taken up again in a later chapter.

After a drive to Caen with Agostinelli at the wheel, Proust wrote an article published by *Le Figaro* in November 1907, "Impressions de route en automobile." This article would make it into his novel with only a few changes. Because it lies at the core of the structure of the novel, its developing storyline of the Narrator becoming a writer will also be discussed in greater detail in this book.

3. *In Search of Lost Time*

The year 1908 was exceptional in the genesis of Proust's novel. Mme Straus gave Proust five notebooks, the largest of which he chose to begin making notes for several projects he had in mind that would, in retrospect, clearly lead to the creation of his novel, including topics, themes, characters, sensations, memories, and dreams. It is known as *Le Carnet de 1908* (*The 1908 Notebook*). Along with it, he wrote a series of *Pastiches* (*Parodies*) of authors that were published in *Le Figaro*, and also began an essay that would eventually be known as *Contre Sainte-Beuve* (*Against Sainte-Beuve*). Taken together, these works made 1908 a good year for Proust, as he began what is now known as *In Search of Lost Time*.

Proust may have lost money in the casino at the Grand-Hôtel, but he was also able to meet several young men there. They were generally from middle-class families and would play varying degrees of importance in Proust's life and in his novel. One of the most interesting was Marcel Plantevignes, whose father was a necktie manufacturer. Proust and Plantevignes (19 at the time) were to become longtime friends despite one notable incident. On a walk one day, Plantevignes stopped to speak to a lady who implied that Proust was a homosexual. Plantevignes said nothing. Word got back to Proust about this and he exploded in a way reminiscent of the way he reacted to the columnist Jean Lorrain regarding his homophobic article about *Pleasures and Days*. He was upset that Plantevignes had not defended him. Again, his honor was in question and, though Plantevignes was not the source, he was clearly hurt that someone he considered a close friend did not speak in his defense. Proust wrote a letter to Plantevignes that alarmed him and his father, who went to see Proust. Proust reacted by challenging him to a duel—just as he challenged Lorrain years earlier. Fortunately, there was a reconciliation between the two men.

There was also another incident involving Plantevignes but, instead of pain, it brought Proust a unique pleasure. Since it also plays such an important role in the novel, we will return to it later. Plantevignes would write an interesting book based on his firsthand knowledge of Proust, *Avec Marcel Proust: Causeries-Souvenirs sur Cabourg et le Boulevard Haussmann* (Marcel Proust: Conversations-Memories from Cabourg and the Boulevard Haussmann).

Proust also encountered other young men at the casino. Some of the traits for Robert de Saint-Loup and Albertine were inspired by two young engineers named Pierre Parent and Max Daireaux. Another young man named Albert Nahmias would become a particularly close friend. It is possible that this group was the inspiration for the "little band of girls" the Narrator encounters in Balbec.

Progressing with the novel

That year, 1908, Proust also faced his doubts and uncertainties directly and, by doing so, would make serious progress in creating his novel. He worried that "Laziness or doubt or impotency [was] taking refuge in the lack of certainty over the art form." For 10 years, he had been in search of everything that *Jean Santeuil* lacked and the answer to the essential question: "Must I make of it a novel, a philosophical study, am I a novelist?" In facing his doubts, he found the answer to what was lacking in his earlier effort. His doubts and uncertainties would become the Narrator's and the search for the answers would become the storyline of the novel.

In late 1908, Proust bought some more notebooks, now like the ones he used as a schoolboy. By August 1909, he had filled 10 of them with a total of 700 pages that would become *Contre Sainte-Beuve*. At 37 years old, Proust was on his way to achieving his goal of becoming a writer and even a novelist, as he wanted. By March 1909, he declared that he had a "full trunk in the middle of my brain [that] hampers me and I must decide whether to set off or to unpack it." He also had a "boy" inside him who "dies instantly in the particular, and begins immediately to float and live in the general.... But while he lives his life is only ecstasy and felicity. He alone should write my books." Perhaps the most fundamental division of Self into a plurality of identities is the division between the social self and the inner, creative self (the "boy" inside him). Fundamental oppositions are being developed. Art breaks "the ice of the habitual and the rational." Involuntary memory takes precedence over voluntary memory as the way to free the "boy" inside. At this point, it is still just the taste of toast and tea that brings back a memory and is placed at the front of the novel. Notes in the drafts for *Contre Sainte-Beuve* contain what would become the decisive conclusion that "Real books should be the offspring not of daylight and casual talk but of darkness and silence." The broad outline of the novel would become apparent sometime between the summers of 1908 and 1909. He was writing a sort of immense novel that, as a Proust biographer William Carter said, is "perhaps the most remarkable example of a sustained narrative in the history of literature."

Proust had planned to have his bedroom walls lined with cork in August 1909 while he was away vacationing at the Grand-Hôtel in Cabourg. Unfortunately, he had not reserved his room, was given another, and was distressed over staying in an unfamiliar room. Unsure whether he could live in a different room or might have to return to Paris early, he canceled the work with the cork. It would not be until the following year that the famous sound-proofed room at 102 boulevard Haussmann would be constructed. The building is now owned by a bank that has an office on the street level. Supposedly, one can visit Proust's apartment on Thursday afternoons, but visits are at the discretion of the person at the front desk.

In 1910, Proust made a lot of progress on his novel. He had both the artistic, intuitive, internal self and the more rational, intellectual self that might have been in control of the regime of expressing and re-creating what he had found. He needed the time and quiet that the sound-proofed room could bring in order for him to work at night and sleep during the day. Looked at from the perspective of what came of it, it was a very practical solution to his problem. Nothing could be allowed to stop the work he was doing. Though he did go out occasionally, he also had to nurture his creative, inner self at the expense of his outer, social self and, in doing so, limit his interaction with people.

The noise was another matter. There was a flood that damaged many buildings, including Proust's basement. Proust's torture was not limited to the resulting construction. A huge pigeon that had gone down the chimney was making a noise in the wall. Proust's aural perimeter was under multiple attacks. The solution to his insomnia was more drugs, including veronal and opium.

Ballets Russes

In 1910, Serge Diaghilev brought his Ballets Russes back to Paris with the production of *Scheherazade* from one of Proust's favorite books, *The Arabian Nights*. With the Ballet, came its choreographer Vaslav Nijinsky, dancer Ida Rubinstein, and composer Igor Stravinsky (who is the subject of another *Simply Charly* book, *Simply Stravinsky*). Proust loved the ballet and soon met Jean Cocteau, already making a name for himself in the art and literary world at 22. Proust's friend, Reynaldo Hahn, was collaborating on a ballet with Cocteau and Federico de Madrazo. Cocteau and Madrazo would write the book for Hahn's ballet, *Le Dieu bleu*, for the Ballets Russes. Along with the innovative Ballets Russes and all the Russian talent that accompanied the troupe, Diaghilev collaborated with some of France's most creative minds, including composers Claude Debussy, Maurice Ravel, Erik Satie, the writer André Gide, the painter Pablo Picasso, and the aforementioned Cocteau and Hahn. Proust not only attended the performances, but also had firsthand knowledge of the most modern currents in the arts in Paris at the time.

At the end of another vacation at the coast, Odilon Albaret drove Proust back to Paris, where he would begin a long and productive period of isolation. By November, he was working on "Swann in Love," the section in *Swann's Way* that follows "Combray." It is a self-contained story in the third person because the Narrator had not yet been born and could not have observed or been part of it. This would prove helpful in Proust's efforts to follow a family through several generations and, like Charles Darwin, Jean-Baptiste Lamarck, and other naturalists, observe traits that might reappear (be they inherited or acquired). Because of the long time frame involved, it is difficult to observe several generations in the human species, but Proust did his best.

Early in 1911, Proust embraced another modern innovation, the "theatrophone," a device allowing people to listen to live theater and opera performances over telephone lines. For a fee, Proust was connected to eight Paris theaters and concert halls through the still relatively new telephone system. The pianola brought another sound system into Proust's closed-in world, when he bought an Aeolian player piano that he attached to his grand piano. His driver Alfred Agostinelli probably encouraged Proust to buy it and Bertrand de Fénelon pumped it for Proust as Albertine would do for the Narrator in the novel. (If you want to see and experience a pianola and some of the music it plays, there is a small pianola museum in the Jordaan area of Amsterdam, just around the corner from the Café Proust.)

Proust's small, enclosed world was now being penetrated in a positive way, bringing indoors what he would have experienced outside, leaving his creative artistic self behind for the social self. Eventually, the former would take control and the few trips he made were in search of material for his novel. He hired a secretary and had written more than 700 pages, but he still had not created the title by which his masterpiece would be known. Soundproofing, drugs, coffee, and home theater and music systems helped make his isolation bearable and his work possible.

A voluminous manuscript

The following year, 1912, marked the expansion of his novel, unsuccessful attempts to have it published, defending it against critics who said it was an autobiography, and explaining to friends that the characters in it were creative fictions. As the manuscript grew, he wondered if it should be published as a single volume of 800 or 900 pages, or two separate books. As it kept growing to 1,400 pages, he debated whether it should be two 700-page volumes or five 300-page volumes. In a letter to Montesquiou, he wrote that he was concerned people might misunderstand his book, "which is so carefully constructed and concentric and which people will mistake for mere childhood memoirs." After a performance at the Opéra Garnier, where he was able to observe two particular dresses that expressed the finest among women's fashions of the *Belle Epoque*, he wrote that "the two women whom I shall dress up in their clothes—like two mannequins—have no connection with them, my novel has no key."

Proust wanted *la Nouvelle Revue Française* (NRF) to publish his novel and offered to pay as much as they desired. During negotiations, he continued working and came up with two titles: *Lost Time* (*Le Temps perdu*) and *Time Regained* (*Le Temps retrouvé*). Although the overall title was not yet complete, the circular nature of the novel was already apparent and the grounds for the search for something lost and eventually rediscovered was established. He also tried to have Fasquelle publish his manuscripts. While the NRF was more respectable, Fasquelle could reach a wider audience, "the sort of people who buy badly printed volumes before catching a train." Proust's goal was never to write a novel for the elite few. However, both publishers rejected his novel. The rejection of the editor at a third publisher, Ollendorf, is quoted in the book's Introduction.

In 1913, *Swann's Way* (*Du côté de chez Swann*) was published at Grasset, at Proust's expense. He even limited his part of the share of any profits so that the volumes might be sold at a cheaper price in the hopes that it would be read by more people. Money was not his motive. Rather, it was "the infiltration of my ideas into the greatest number of brains susceptible of receiving them." The importance to Proust of a receptive reader is apparent from the beginning of the first year of publication. In the same year, 1913, he also decided on *Le Côté de Guermantes* and the overall title took its final French form, *À la recherche du temps perdu*.

As the novel kept growing, Proust told Jacques Copeau, a French theater director, that "by reading myself I've discovered after the event some of the constituent elements of my own unconscious." Responding to concerns about the homosexuality and sadism that appear in his novel, he defended their inclusion as one of scientific objectivity: "I obey a general truth which forbids me to appeal to sympathetic souls any more than to antipathetic ones ... it cannot alter the terms in which I probe the truth and which are not determined by my personal whim." He wrote about what he saw in himself and in others without the filters that social norms would impose, restricting and altering his observations. Not to have done so would have invalidated his search for the laws that govern man, ending his quest for the essence of man and world.

There were also changes in his household personnel that would prove decisive, both in Proust's life and in his novel. Alfred Agostinelli had lost his job as a driver, so Proust hired him as his secretary. Proust was extremely generous with Agostinelli, paying for his flying lessons. He had his other driver, Odilon, drive Agostinelli to Buc, where Roland Garros (the first person to fly across the Mediterranean) had an aviation school. Apparently tired of typing and moving about in the small, enclosed world of his employer, he thought of going to a flying school on the Riviera. The "artisan of my voyage" in 1907 had now become the "companion

In Search of Lost Time | 27

of my captivity," and Proust may have offered Agostinelli a Rolls-Royce or an airplane if he would stay with him in Paris. Odilon married a young woman from his village named Céleste Gineste. In November, Céleste started coming regularly to Proust's home to work from nine to five, while Proust slept. Due to bad investments, the expenses incurred during the process of publishing *Du côté de chez Swann*, and lavish presents for Agostinelli, Proust's wealth and health both declined.

Critiques and praise

Proust was still haunted by some of the critiques that followed his publication of *Pleasures and Days*. The adjectives that were often used, "delicate" and "sensitive," were particularly distasteful to Proust, and the publication of *Swann's Way* deserved "living and true" instead. He was already afraid that the length of the novel might be a barrier to some readers but explained that "it is the invisible substance of time that I have tried to isolate, and it meant that the experiment had to last over a long period." It is not only distance the reader must traverse in the world Proust had created, she or he must also travel in time. *Swann's Way* was also quickly seen as a masterpiece by many critics and writers, including Jean Cocteau, who wrote that it "resembles nothing I know and everything that I admire." Other French writers also praised the work. Lucien Daudet wrote: "Never, I believe, has the analysis of everything that constitutes our existence been carried so far." Francis Jammes called Proust "the equal of Shakespeare and Balzac." Maurice Rostand published a review in which he referred to *Swann's Way* as "a soul in the guise of a book." But where Cocteau saw an original composition, others only saw *de*composition, lacking plot and structure, and not belonging to any particular genre. Proust referred to his fictional musical composer and genius, Vinteuil, when writing to a critic, "Isn't that composition?" Jazz must have sounded like that to those who were only used to classical music. When Proust wrote one of his long sentences in his long book or reintroduced a character, theme, or thought, unexpected, underlying patterns would become apparent. An incredible, new structure was there, but not everyone had the eyes to see its beauty or–to follow the musical analogy–the ears to hear it. In their defense, Proust had only begun and the readers at the time were not able to experience his work in its entirety.

In 1914, the *Belle Epoque* ended, and World War I began. Proust did not have to serve in the military, as his name had been taken off the list of those who were fit. Odilon, however, had been drafted and Céleste moved into Proust's home. The publishing of Proust's novel had ceased due to the lack of men and the fact that lead used for printing in those days was needed for the war effort. But Proust kept on writing. He chose *Sodom and Gomorrah* as the title of the fourth part of his novel, with Sodom representing male homosexuals and Gomorrah symbolizing lesbians. Both play a significant role in the novel, as do bisexuals and a lot of uncertainty regarding the sexuality of some of his characters. The novel grew, but the circular nature and the essential themes, patterns, and ideas, remained intact. During the war years, from 1914 to 1918, Proust's novel grew from about half a million words to approximately 1.25 million words. Much of it had to do with the development of the object of the Narrator's obsessive love, Albertine, and with her jealousy, sex, death, memory, time, and, eventually, inescapable solitude. Events and experiences related to the war were also included.

An "upside down" life

In 1915, hundreds of thousands of Frenchmen died in the war. Blackouts in Paris had been ordered because of the German attacks. During this time, Proust met a young diplomat, Paul Morand, who knew Bertrand de Fénelon and saw much of him in the fictional

Robert de Saint-Loup. Céleste, the only remaining member of Proust's household other than himself, described their life as a "sort of upside-down and almost completely closed world where we seemed to have our own special calendar ... and our own clock whose hours were dictated by M. Proust and had nothing to do with other people's hours." She provided many services, but her help with his revisions and proofs was truly remarkable. She had no trouble resolving Proust's problems with the additions and corrections he was making, causing confusion for his editor. She suggested he leave some space on his changes and she would "stick them as carefully as I can at the right place. In that way you can add as much as you like, all we have to do is fold the paper. Then the printer will have to unfold the strips ... in the right order." Proust loved the idea. One of her "paste-ons" reached nearly one-and-a-half meters.

During this time, Jacques-Emile Blanche, who had previously painted Proust's portrait, said he would read the proofs of the growing novel, to which Proust replied that he could read them but not in his presence: "I live on the surface of myself and it is only when I am alone that I redescend into the hole in which I see somewhat clearly."

Proust was always hungry for as much information about the world and the people that inhabit it as he could get. What he found out through salons, exhibits, books, friends, family, working people, and his own experiences has already been noted. But the allure of gossip, of layers of dissimulation that could be penetrated only by knowing where to go and whom to pay to find out what was going on, was of particular interest to Proust. One of the many "small enclosed worlds" that Proust was able to penetrate was that of the Ritz. Olivier Dabescat's restaurant at the Ritz served as elite a clientele then as it continues to do so today (made famous to many when Princess Diana left from there before her tragic accident). Proust had become a regular at the Ritz, getting food and information through Dabescat, and from some of the waiters he got to know. A second and even more "enclosed and diverse world" was made available to Proust by Albert Le Cuziat, who ran a male brothel and baths. The dissimulation inherent to both (though obviously for different reasons) made them particularly appealing to Proust. We shall return to its fictional counterpart, Jupien's male brothel, in a later chapter, though it is important to discuss here how anyone knew anything about this side of Proust's life that he hid to the point of dueling. Proust had to be careful at Le Cuziat's establishment, as it was often raided. Thanks to Le Cuziat, Proust had a peephole through which he could observe without being observed. Some have called this "voyeurism" and there is likely some truth to this. The trite excuse for being in a place of "ill repute" is that one is doing research. However, in Proust's case, this was at least in part true. When Proust arrived home from Le Cuziat's brothel he would recount in detail to Céleste what he had seen, "just as if he'd come back from an evening at the Comte de Beaumont's or Comtesse Greffulhe's." Proust's stories must have made quite an impression on this young woman from the country. When she told Proust that she did not understand why he went to the brothel, he replied, "I know, Céleste. You can't imagine how much I dislike it. But I can only write things as they are, and to do that I have to see them." One may have doubts, but the scientist in Proust is evident here. One time he told her that what he had seen was "unimaginable." He had watched as an industrialist from the north of France was being whipped while chained, with lots of blood everywhere. Céleste asked, "And did you have to pay a lot of money to see it?" Proust's reply: "Yes, Céleste. But I had to."

    Evidence (germ phobia and probable impotency from all the drugs he was taking) make the stories about his masturbating with no physical contact plausible. The only known firsthand story is from an anonymous male prostitute who said that there was no contact and Proust was evidently masturbating under the covers. To some friends, Proust's appreciation of young men appeared to be platonic and this event could hardly be described as a passionate relationship. But there is no certainty, no known, evidentiary light to be shed on this subject. Peering through Proust's peephole, either to look into his own sexual practices or to find out his means of knowing what he wrote about, is difficult for a biographer for obvious reasons. It is thanks in large part to Céleste that anything is known about the source that would lead to the apocalyptic yet darkly humorous scene in wartime Paris at Jupien's male brothel in *Time Regained*.

A "novel with its strong structure and sturdy foundation"

In 1916, Proust attended some of the concerts being given in Paris where he was able to hear Beethoven, Franck, Fauré, Mozart, Schumann, and Wagner being played. The Narrator's thoughts on music in general and his fictional composer, Vinteuil, in particular, came from attending these concerts. (While the "little phrase" of music comes from Saint-Saëns, Proust was not a great fan.) One night, Proust rounded up the members of the Poulet Quartet. He had heard them play Franck's Quartet in D and wanted to hear it again that night. By 1 a.m. he had the members in his bedroom. They were well paid to play it again—twice—and Céleste brought them champagne and fried potatoes before they took the cabs in the early dawn that Proust had ordered for them. The sound-proofed, cork-lined walls helped keep the sound in rather than keeping the noise out. Music aided both Proust and his Narrator on their quest into the darkness of one's self. Music shows "us what richness, what variety lies hidden, unknown to us, in that vast, unfathomed and forbidding night of our soul which we take to be an impenetrable void."

During this period, Proust was finally courted by the publisher he originally wanted and, with some time and effort, he switched from Grasset to Gallimard. His fear of dying before he finished his novel continued. One of the most touching moments in a documentary that was done for French television (and is included in William Carter's documentary on Proust) is an interview with Céleste where she describes one afternoon around 4 p.m. when she went to Proust's bedroom and saw the radiant joy in his face. Even more telling, for the first time, he spoke to her before having his first coffee of the day. He told her he had wonderful news, that "something tremendous. Something so wonderful" had happened:

> He sat up in bed, smiled at me and said "I have written 'The End.' Now I can die."
>
> So I said to him "But what about all the bits of paper I still have to paste together? And all the corrections you still have to make?"
>
> "That, my dear, that's something else."

This did not mean that Proust was finished working on his novel. But if he were to die, it would stand as a novel with its strong structure and sturdy foundation. Céleste says it happened in 1922, but it could have happened as early as 1916.

In 1917 there were threats growing from without and from within. The Germans were still approaching Paris with their modern weaponry, and Proust was still dealing with his ailments. His insomnia continued, with one 50-hour stretch with no sleep causing Proust to compare himself to Graham, a character in H. G. Wells's novel, *When the Sleeper Wakes*. Proust still managed to go out and often had dinner with Morand and Cocteau at Princess Soutzo's apartment at the Ritz. After one dinner, there was a session with a hypnotist. Proust also attended an extraordinary and modern cultural event at the Théâtre du Châtelet. Cocteau's ballet *Parade* had modern choreography by Léonide Massine and music by Erik Satie, who used typewriters and sirens, along with other modern sounds. Thanks to Picasso's debut as a set and costume designer, Cubist art was seen for the first time in a theater. The poet and playwright Guillaume Apollinaire coined the term *surréaliste* for the ballet's program notes.

By the end of January 1918, the Germans made their first air attack on Paris using their new bombers, called Gothas. They were also bombarding Paris with their new and deadly cannons manufactured by the Krupps family called Berthas. At the same time, Proust's own internal threats were also growing. He was having trouble speaking and was afraid it was facial paralysis. He wrote a friend that he was planning to see Dr. Joseph Babinski, a neurologist who had studied with Jean-Martin Charcot, a French neurologist who worked on hypnosis and hysteria. Eventually, paralysis was ruled out in favor of another diagnosis–taking too many narcotics. In June, Proust sent Gallimard the corrected proofs for *Within a Budding Grove* and the manuscript of *The Guermantes Way*. On Monday, November 11, the war ended and on November 30, the printer finished *Within a Budding Grove* (A l'ombre des jeunes filles en fleurs).

4. Final Years

In January 1919, Proust received the proofs for *Pastiches et Mélanges*, a new edition of *Swann's Way*, and an advance copy of *Within a Budding Grove*. But it was not a great year in Proust's personal life. Never a fan of moving, the sale of his residence on boulevard Haussmann resisted by his Aunt Amélie Weil was a catastrophe for Proust. It was bought by a banker, who forgave Proust's overdue rent, paid him three years' rent, and also included some cash. According to Céleste, "Death began for him with our leaving boulevard Haussmann." Proust and Céleste first moved to rue Laurent-Pichat, then to what would be his last home, 44, rue Hamelin.

In addition to progress in publishing his novel, Proust was receiving accolades and awards. Comte Jean de Gaigneron compared Proust's book to a cathedral. This was a nice surprise since Proust had not told anyone about this: "I have wanted to give to each part of my book the title: Portal I: Stained Glass Windows of the Apse, etc., to answer in advance the stupid criticism ... over the lack of construction in a book where I will show that the only merit is in the solidity of the most minor parts." He did not pursue this idea because it was "too pretentious." Francis Jammes had asked Proust to cut out the lesbian-sadist scene of Evil between Mlle Vinteuil and her friend at Montjouvain. In a letter to François Mauriac, he explained that he would be happy to satisfy Jammes's request, "but I had constructed this work so carefully that this episode in the first volume explains the jealousy of my young man in the fourth and fifth volumes so that by ripping out the column with the obscene capital, I would have brought down the arch. That's what critics like to call works without composition and written according to random memories." It could be said that Proust gambled by putting everything into the success (or lack thereof) of one novel. It is easy to say in hindsight that it would be a masterpiece, but it took great conviction, even courage in the face of the many criticisms and difficulties, along with a lot of hard work and sacrifice. But Proust knew art, literature, and philosophy. He knew that his vision, albeit innovative and even shocking, was important, despite whatever financial, critical, social, or health costs it might entail. Proust was honest. What he saw was true and real, and he would not sacrifice any part of his edifice to anything other than a complete reflection of his vision.

On Wednesday, December 10, Proust was awarded France's highest literary prize, the *Prix Goncourt* for *Within a Budding Grove*. Numerous and important critics praised its psychological analysis. Acceptance, awards, and praise were pouring in, but by this time Proust was spending most of his time in bed, still working on his novel. The combination of the two moves he had to make and an ever-increasing dependence on drugs—including at least five stimulants and depressants—did not help.

The new decade

In 1920, Proust won more awards, used more drugs, and received growing international recognition. He was named *Chevalier de la légion d'honneur*, the highest French medal of honor. Marcel Proust Societies were formed in several countries, including Holland, Belgium, and England. With only the first two volumes of *In Search of Lost Time* published, critics were already talking about how he had created a new world. Later in the same year, he published *Le Côté de Guermantes I* (*The Guermantes Way I*). The editor of *La Nouvelle Revue Française* Jacques Rivière thought it would amuse Proust to know that "André Breton, the head Dadaist, came to help us correct your proofs and delivered to me an intense admiration for you based on the poetic treasures he discovered in your work." Proust appreciated the compliment but was not impressed with the job such excellent readers as Rivière and the "charming Dadaist" had done. After reading the third volume of *In Search of Lost Time*, Lucien Daudet wrote that it was a "psychological manual more complex than all the others, a totally new artistic 'doctrine' and the most amusing of all novels.... You have re-created the novel, and you are the greatest novelist who has ever lived in any epoch in any country." Still unable to sleep, Proust's problems with drugs increased. He evidently took a whole box of Veronal, along with opium and some other medications aimed at fighting his nocturnal existence. Not only did it not help, it almost killed him. He went for two days without ringing for Céleste.

Despite all this, in December Proust wrote two individuals with comments that showed a level of clarity of vision with an equally clear–and succinct–expression of it. We shall look at the second of these in the following chapter, since the letter sent to a French journalist Louis Martin-Chauffier pertains to the Narrator and the fundamental role he plays in the novel. The first comment was to a French poet and critic, Emile Henriot, and was a brief answer to a survey on classic and romantic writers. He wrote that he believed that "all true art is classical, but the laws of the mind rarely permit it to be, when it first appears, as such." His examples came from the pictorial arts with Edouard Manet's *Olympia* and literature, with Baudelaire's *The Flowers of Evil* (*Les Fleurs du mal*). At the time (and still today, for that matter) their innovative creations were a shock and hardly seen as "classic." Proust wrote that "innovators worthy of becoming classics one day obey a strict inner discipline and are builders above all. But precisely because their architecture is new, it takes a long time for people to discern it." One might add, especially if it has not yet been published in its entirety.

Controversy over *Sodom and Gomorrah*

On January 11, 1921, Proust wrote Gallimard a letter describing his poor physical health (bronchitis and a high fever), the remaining four volumes to be published, and asking about the royalties he was owed. By May, Proust's health had worsened but *The Guermantes Way II* (*Le Côté de Guermantes II*) and *Sodom and Gomorrah I* (*Sodome et Gomorrhe I*) were available for publication. Proust was criticized by those who were upset over the discussion of homosexuality. French journalist and writer Léon Daudet, older brother of Lucien, told Proust he could not even mention the title *Sodome et Gomorrhe* to his readers. At the same time, it did not matter that he was trying to be objective, the result of his "impartial point of view, that of a true naturalist," was also offensive to many homosexuals. André Gide was among the most important and most vocal of those who considered his descriptions unfair. Proust covered a broad spectrum of human sexuality with a depth and precision that had not been seen before and it caused reactions from individuals who saw too close of a resemblance with themselves, to religious and other conservative groups, and homosexuals who took offense at the sometimes less-than-heroic descriptions.

On April 21, the Jeu de Paume had an exhibition of Dutch masters. In order to make this daytime visit and go to the Hôtel des Antiquaires et des Beaux Arts to see some paintings by Jean-Auguste-Dominique Ingres, Proust again simply did not go to bed the night before. The last photograph of Proust was taken of him standing on the terrace next to the Jeu de Paume after seeing the Dutch masters which, thanks to Paul Morand, included Proust's favorite painting, Vermeer's *View of Delft*. He is well dressed, standing very straight, and looking gloriously happy, especially given his poor health, overuse of narcotics and other drugs, and continuing insomnia. In the scene that precedes his fictional author Bergotte's death, he has just seen this same Vermeer painting. Before he faints and dies in the museum, he realizes the limits of his own writing compared to just one part of the painting, the "little patch of yellow wall." In a question similar to the one the Narrator poses at the beginning of the novel about his memories of Combray, just before he tastes the madeleine and tea ("Dead forever? It was possible"), the Narrator asks if Bergotte is "Dead forever? Who can say?" After the fictional author's burial, "all through that night of mourning, in the lighted shop windows, his books, arranged three by three, kept vigil like angels with outspread wings and seemed for him who was no more, the symbol of his resurrection." In neither quotation is there evidence of a belief in the afterlife—religious or otherwise. Nor is there a negation of it. There is only uncertainty. After the former quotation, however, there does appear to be hope in the "special pleasure" coming from the experience with the madeleine and tea. The first section of "Combray" ends with a beautiful, crescendo-like sentence, in which everyone and everything that was thought dead and gone "sprang into being ... from my cup of tea." We shall return to the importance of this privileged moment later. As for the second quotation regarding the question of death, the description of Bergotte's books leaves the possibility of an afterlife open. Both are based on his aesthetic theories, and not on a religious belief.

Worsening health and death

In May 1922, *Sodome et Gomorrhe II* was published, but the year marked increasingly poor health, more drugs, financial difficulties, and isolation in the limited sphere of his last home at rue Hamelin. Proust's germ phobia had increased to the point that his mail had to be passed through a chamber that contained formaldehyde before he would touch it. He was taking dangerous amounts of adrenaline, both by injection and dry. On May 1, he took the dry form in a dose so strong that it burned his digestive tract to the point that he ate and drank almost nothing afterward except ice cream and iced beer from the Ritz. In June, he admitted he was spending too much money on ice cream.

In May, Proust managed to attend a late-night supper at the Hôtel Majestic in the presence of the most modern artists, composers, and writers of his time. Included were Diaghilev, Picasso and his wife, and Irish novelist James Joyce. Neither Proust nor Joyce had read much, if any, of the other writer's work. Proust never mentioned their encounter, but Joyce wrote that "Proust would only talk about duchesses, while I was more concerned with their chambermaids." After the event at the Hôtel Majestic, Joyce tried to continue the party at Proust's home, but Proust managed to escape his inebriated fellow writer. In October, Joyce wrote that he had "read the first two volumes recommendés by [the British novelist] Mr. [Sydney] Schiff of A la Recherche des Ombrelles Perdues par Plusieurs Jeunes Filles en Fleurs du Côté de chez Swann et Gomorrhée et Co. par Marcelle Proyce and James Joust." Based on this sentence alone it should be safe to say that Joyce saw some of himself in Proust.

In September, Proust was so weak that he had to take an injection of anti-asthma medication combined with stimulants just to be able to work for an hour. He was worn down to the point that, "deprived of everything, my only care is to give my [books], through their absorption by other minds, the expansion that is refused me." By late October, Proust's asthma and coughing were getting worse, but he refused treatment even from his brother (a doctor), Reynaldo Hahn, Odilon, and Céleste. After developing bronchitis and pneumonia, Proust died on November 22. Cocteau described the stack of notebooks on Proust's mantel: "That pile of paper on his left was still alive, like watches ticking on the wrists of dead soldiers." He phoned the avant-garde photographer Man Ray to come and photograph Proust on his deathbed. Funeral services were held at the church of Saint-Pierre de Chaillot. Proust's friends evidently did not notice James Joyce who, hidden in the crowd, had come to pay his respects. After a long funeral procession across Paris, Proust was buried in the family plot at Père-Lachaise cemetery.

In January 1923, *Vanity Fair* published in America the first photograph of Proust, taken by the photographer Nadar in 1896. *Sodome et Gomorrhe III–La Prisonnière* (*The Captive*) was published. In 1924, *Albertine disparue* (*The Fugitive*) was published, and in 1927

Le Temps retrouvé (Time Regained). His watches were still ticking. The absorption into other minds continues thanks to the receptive readers who have felt included in his quest.

5. The Narrator: Travels in the Space-Time Continuum

Who is the Narrator in the novel and what is his name? What do we know about him and how do we know it? Because of the mixture of real people, events, and places with imaginary ones, and because we see the genesis of the novel and the role of the Narrator in Proust's notebooks and other sources, we know he drew from his own experiences to create the Narrator.

And who else could have given him the direct observations of reality, from particular details to general laws, other than himself? Into whose consciousness (and unconscious) could he have gone to explore man's internal world, if not his own? The exceptionally close relationship between the author and the Narrator is clear. But to say that the Narrator is Proust would be incorrect. Proust was a person. The Narrator is a character in a novel. Proust's own writings in what would be *Contre Sainte-Beuve,* in his novel and elsewhere, make it clear that one cannot look at the Narrator as if he were a reflection of the author. He is a creation from the author's imagination, and the distinction is important. The truly inclusive and expansive relationship resides between the Narrator and the reader. The Narrator is shown as a reader himself on the first page of the novel, and not as a writer. The desire to be a writer is soon evident and its gradual realization is an essential part of the novel, but it is not until the very end that his goal is going to be achieved. In the first sentence, we learn that he (French grammar shows that the Narrator is a man) used to go to bed early (and consequently does not anymore). We then learn that he has fallen asleep while reading and "it seemed to me that I myself was the immediate subject of my book: a church, a quartet, the rivalry between François I and Charles V." We learn more about the book he is reading and his becoming a part of it before we learn anything about when, where, or even who, the Narrator is. When he wakes up enough to pull himself out of the worlds of sleep, he looks outward, seeing only darkness.

What is the Narrator's name? For a long time, he was generally referred to as "Marcel" or, in the first of many divisions, the young Narrator being recalled and going through the experiences is "Marcel," using "Narrator" for the older insomniac or the "omniscient" character (which are not necessarily always the same). Though the name "Marcel" is used to refer to the Narrator, it only occurs twice in the novel. Both are in the fifth volume, *The Captive*, and both involve Albertine. In the first instance, she is in "the uncertainty of awakening and says 'My–' or 'My darling–' followed by my Christian name, which, if we give the narrator the same name as the author of this book, would be 'My Marcel,' or 'My darling Marcel.'" In an interesting reflection of the Narrator's options regarding his name, Albertine might use "Marcel" in the uncertain moments of awakening. But only if "we" give the same name to the Narrator of "this book" as its author. Both the attribution of "this book" and the pronoun "we" are unusual and, while the first focuses the reader's vision on the fictional book in hand, the pronoun expands the decision-making power to someone beyond the Narrator, presumably the reader. The barriers separating the realities of the Narrator, the Author, and the Reader appear to be cracking. It is also possible that Proust simply did not get to finish his corrections on this part of the novel and would have changed it and the second reference to the Narrator as Marcel, which occurs shortly after. In a letter to the Narrator, Albertine begins by using the same "charming expression": "'My darling dear Marcel,'" and ends with "'What a Marcel! What a Marcel!'" Proust himself participated in this blurring of identities by referring to the Narrator as "I" in letters and notes, despite his aesthetical theories that emphasize the distinction between the Author and his creation. But what dominates the other 3000+ pages of the novel is the very anonymity of the Narrator: we do not know his name or what he looks like.

The mysterious Narrator

Is there one singular Narrator, or should he be referred to in the plural? The differences between the old insomniac remembering the past and the young Narrator going through the remembered experiences is one division. Another, equally clear division is made between the "social self" that operates on a superficial, outward-looking level and the "creative self" that is turned inward, toward the depths of one's essence. But the divisions do not stop here. Like Swann, we learn who he is by how he is perceived in and reflected by, the world. The Narrator's multiplication into a plurality of identities occurs through time, throughout the novel. He is a variable connected to the constant of wanting to be a writer/novelist. His love interests bring out numerous and varied Narrators, as if he were a kaleidoscope that, while made up of the same pieces, creates different patterns based on which way it is turned and the light shining (or not) onto it. For simplicity's sake, we shall simply use "Narrator." The very vagueness of the disembodied voice of the nebulous Narrator in the opening pages allows the reader to become part of the book even more easily than what the Narrator experiences. There is no name, no description to limit the reader from becoming part of Proust's novel, from joining in the Narrator's quest and even seeing it through his eyes as if they were one's own, blurring the boundaries separating the reality of the novel and that of the reader.

Proust's novel is far from being a walled-in fortress guarded by an intellectual or any other elite. The Narrator could not be a more welcoming host. Not only does he present himself in the same activity as the reader, with no particulars to distinguish himself, but he also helps bring the reader on an adventure as magical and exciting as the stories told in *The Arabian Nights*. Like Abou Hassan in "The Story of the Awakened Sleeper," the Narrator opens his door to strangers, inviting them in for a feast (resulting in a change in identity, to which we shall return). Like Scheherazade, the Narrator must tell his stories and leave the listener/reader wanting more in order to survive. Like Aladdin and his magic carpet, he has a "magic chair [that] will carry him at full speed through time and space," on an adventure that can include the receptive Reader who is ready to ride.

Like Proust, the Narrator is known for his sedentary existence, confined to his room, or moving in the closed world of the salons. He does get up and around, however, at times picking up enough speed to experience the unsettling feeling of a world in motion. No longer is one anchored in a stable universe based on rational, causal principles. The Cartesian and Newtonian mechanical universe, open to rational, conscious observation, is left behind for an Einsteinian universe, in which space is confounded with time, causality is replaced by statistical probability, and conscious, rational observation no longer precedes theory formation in the search for truth. The Narrator's quest can be said to have taken him down Heraclitus's river into Einsteinian eddies in the space-time continuum.

The succession of the Narrator's experiences is a mirror image of those of the Narrator's Aunt Léonie–the former knowing increasing mobility in a movement outward (with occasional periods of confinement, like keeping Albertine "a prisoner" in Paris and his own confinement in a health facility)–the latter, increasing immobility in an inward movement: "first Combray, then her house in Combray, then her bedroom, and finally her bed..." Her state of inertia has led her to a state of complete uncertainty as to the objective validity of the information brought to her by her senses. Both the origin of the information and the possibility of its objective verification by another is in doubt: "In the next room I heard my aunt talking quietly to herself .... in the absolute inertia which she led she attached to the least of her sensations an extraordinary importance. Lacking anyone to confide in–she announced them to herself in a perpetual monologue that was her only form of activity."

Like memory, travel is fundamental to an understanding of Proust's novel. As with memory, inertia is broken. The laws of time and space are destroyed, and a new law, a new order, a new certainty are created. Travel takes the Narrator out of his confinement and his isolation. Novelty replaces habit. Things and places—heretofore separated into little "closed vases"—are reunited. Space itself undergoes a sort of metamorphosis. As memory brings together events isolated in time, so travel—equally as magically—brings together places and people isolated in space. In both cases—in the internal, subjective travel of memory in time and in physical travel in space—he is able to escape the paralyzing inertia and uncertainty experienced by his aunt. His "least sensations" are not experienced in isolation. He finds them instead in the outside world, endowing them with a more objective validity.

For the Narrator, the automobile means many things, not the least of which is his ability to visit more places with Albertine in one day than they could have before in two. Time and space have changed for them. The Narrator explains to Albertine that "distances are only the relationship between time and space and vary with it." Speed, the automobile, the road—all these are essential to Proust's modern vision of the world, memory, the artistic process, and the Narrator's vocation.

The Einsteinian connection

The first popular edition of Albert Einstein's theory came out in 1916 and, as his correspondence with the mathematician Camille Vettard shows, Proust was familiar with the physicist's views. Both the scientist and the novelist saw in the railroad train a vehicle universal enough to serve as an expression of their relative world views. In his work, *Relativity: The Special and the General Theory*, Einstein used the train as a basis for his "clear explanation that anyone can understand." In the chapter entitled "Space and Time in Classical Mechanics," he defined "the purpose of mechanics [which] is to describe how bodies change their position in space with 'time.'"

He explained his theory by questioning the notions of "positions" and "space." If a stone is dropped from a moving train, "do the 'positions' traversed by the stone lie 'in reality' on a straight line or a parabola? Moreover, what is meant by 'motion in space?'" His definitions of position and space, which he founded on classical, Euclidean geometry have been eroded, the "rigid body" they depended on has become fluid, unfixed, the classical, mechanical world, unhinged. With the experience of riding in a train, man's most elementary notions of time and space are shaken. Space is irrelevant; only the time to get there matters.

There is no causal connecting principle in Proust's world. A stereoscopic vision is evident in both time and space, and is of such a fundamental and universal nature as to be called by Belgian literary critic Georges Poulet, paradoxically, "a general principle of discontinuity." This principle is not limited to time and space, but it also applies to the human condition and carries no certainty, no solid, unifying "help from above" in its universal and inescapable impossibility of a happiness found in love. The subject of love is in one place, the object of love in another. The "little enclosed worlds" referred to earlier apply to people, moments, and places alike. The principle of discontinuity, of separation, with its inherent lack of any causal connecting principle, is universal. Yet, is there no connecting principle, no order, no certainty? Perhaps coincidence, or synchronicity, or an acausal connecting principle may suggest such a reordering of the world. It is just such a chance occurrence that brings about the Narrator's experience of the "special pleasure," as when he tastes the madeleine and tea or sees the steeples of Martinville and Vieuxvicq.

Einstein pursued the analogy of the train, adding conceptual problems in the form of varying points of reference, beyond that of the relatively simple platform and a moving train, such as a flying raven and two events on the train viewed by someone on the embankment—are they simultaneous with reference to everyone?

As the Narrator so painfully points out in his theories concerning love, one does not even have the fixed referent of an embankment, as the 'other' is in a state of mobility equal to that of the Narrator. Both the subject, with its own multiplicity of selves, and the object of love, with its inherently uncertain and ever-changing nature, lead the Narrator to experience the anguish of jealousy instead of the security of love. The development of his relationship with Albertine is, in essence, a description of this fundamental Proustian reality. The Narrator is painfully aware that he can never truly know the 'real' Albertine. Not only can he never find out what she is doing and with whom she is doing it, but he also cannot even escape the confines of his own temporal context. As Einstein explained, events which are simultaneous with reference to one coordinate system (such as on a train) are not simultaneous with regard to another coordinate system (such as on an embankment).

The advent of aviation

The introduction of airplanes occurs on a large scale in the last volume, *Time Regained*. World War I had precipitated the use of the airplane. The Narrator is conscious of its intrusion into the one area of apparent stability and unchanging order to which man has looked since the time of the Babylonians—the stars. The Narrator's interest in the beauty of the airplanes' ascent and their inclusion in the celestial clockwork is only surmounted by their breaking of these laws, by their moving and, hence, the destruction of the immutable, unchanging order of the cosmos.

It is no longer only the immediate physical world that is in movement; now the stars and the sky are as well. The personification has reached outward to the limits of the visible universe. The stars are like insects or "human shooting stars." Instead of drawing order, meaning, and certainty down from the heavens, man's ordering reason is projected upward in the form of spotlights and airplanes. The familiarity of an old and unchanging sky is also replaced by the beauty seen in the novelty of the planes. The feeling of security that was previously found in a stable, unchanging universe is replaced by confidence in man's intelligence, his will, and their manifestations on the macrocosmic level in the form of the government and the military. These willful, intellectual intrusions into the sky, while bringing a certain sense of security, are still unsettling, making the Narrator feel he is not even in the same world. It is as if the earth has moved under his feet, as if he were in a different part of the world, under "new stars," where the sky is in more motion than the earth.

   Later, driving in the streets of Paris, faced with the destruction of the world he used to know and all the novelty, all the change, and the unfamiliar surroundings that had earlier brought on so much anguish, the Narrator experiences another of those sudden, magical feelings that transform the world. Change, motion, novelty: all the things that previously brought on uncertainty and fear are now accepted. He uses the experience of driving in an automobile to explain the sensation. It is the experience of a fundamental change of the world he is moving in. The ground on which his automobile is rolling changes from paving stones (divided, as are time and space in the world view just described) into a finer, smoother ride on sand, or dead leaves. Time and space are no longer divided into little parcels. The self is no longer contained and isolated. It is one continuous ride, the "general principle of discontinuity" has been transcended, and the chains of the contingencies of a world fixed in a mechanistic universe are broken. In an inverted image of flight, the Narrator moves from the automobile to the airplane and uses the latter not to suggest death, but rather the resurrecting flight of memory. The different modes of travel used to move about in the external, physical world are also used to describe the Narrator's journey into the unconscious. In this internal world of the self, the traveler must find a new methodology, a new set of tools and standards in his search for certainty in this world, where the observer and the observed have become one. The Narrator's experiences of cars, trains, and planes provide the means by which he achieves this quest.

Motion and travel

Contrary to what one might expect, then, on encountering the sedentary Narrator of the first pages of *Swann's Way*, motion is a fundamental aspect of Proust's novel. The Narrator must travel. As technology develops, so does the individual's relationship to the world. Time and space take on a new meaning as one moves from carriage to train to automobile to airplane. As the Narrator reaches the speed of the train and automobile, he finds the world to be as unfamiliar and in motion as in the first pages of the novel, waking up in the night with no clear sense of time or space. Not only does the Narrator not find certainty, but he ends up in the Einsteinian worldview of relativity. The outward search for certainty, life, science, and technology leads to uncertainty and, as seen in the apocalyptic passage with the airplanes in wartime Paris, to death. Paradoxically, at each experience of speed, of novelty, another brick is laid for his "immense edifice of memory"–the foundation for the Narrator's new certainty. His experiences in the world arouse the "special pleasure," transporting him into the world of the self, outside the contingencies of time and space, where he finds the essence of a new worldview, a new certainty. The previously apocalyptic airplane represents the magical, resurrecting flight of memory and, in the final analysis, the artist himself.

6. A Search for Certainty

In the first four pages of *In Search of Lost Time*, there is a metaphorical description of the void and confusion from which the quest for the lost realities of time, space, and self begins. An insomniac, the Narrator wakes up in the middle of the night so disoriented he does not even know who he is. Feeling "more destitute than a cave dweller," he has "only the most rudimentary sense of existence, such as may lurk and flicker in the depths of an animal's consciousness." Having stripped him of his identity, sleep—and its absence—has carried him back to man's beginnings. In fact, it has reduced him to the core of existence itself. But sleep has also carried away his furniture, his room, everything of which he was only "an insignificant part and whose insensibility [he] would very soon return to share." He has fallen into "the abyss of non-being" from which, he says, he could never escape by himself. Memory arrives to pull him out of the abyss and is already working to rebuild "the original components of [his] self." Memory, already a companion in the search, has only begun the foundation for what will become "the immense edifice of memory" that, as the Narrator will discover, actually holds the very treasure that he has lost.

In the same few opening pages, with the loss of an internal, subjective reality founded on a solid notion of self, the Narrator also loses the external reality of an objective world anchored in fixed notions of time and space: "When a man is asleep, he has in a circle around him the chain of hours, the sequence of the years, the order of the heavenly host." If the chain had held, he would not have needed the help that memory brings. The "kaleidoscope of darkness" that surrounds him is even less a source of certainty than the illusory projections of his magic lantern onto the walls of a childhood bedroom. The realities of subject and object are, in fact, bound together, but it is the latter that depends on the former for a solid foundation rather than the reverse: "Perhaps the immobility of the things that surround us is forced upon them by our conviction that they are themselves and not anything else, by the immobility of our conception of them." A tension has already been established between the subjective, internal world of sleep and dreams, and the objective, external world of conscious order that, according to Richard Bales, the editor of *The Cambridge Companion to Proust*, "endows the unconscious life with a validity which almost, if not indeed totally, equates it with the world of wakefulness." The search for the essence of the one, then, is also the search for the essence of the other. In penetrating the essence of his lost self, the lost reality of the objective world will also be revealed. Memory holds two lost treasures.

Bridging the gap between science and art

The Narrator's movement outward, into the world indicated by the "raised finger of the day" traced on his wall by a ray of light through the almost-closed curtains at the end of "Combray," will provide the necessary ingredients for a successful quest. The outward, telescopic motion then turns inward, focusing on the essence of man. Using the sciences throughout the search, trying to penetrate the essence of the nature of the world and his physical being, the search outward coincides with a movement towards man's internal landscape, or his psyche. Some critics have accused Proust of being "pseudo-scientific." Nonetheless, Proust melded together the most recent developments in science to create the world of his novel. His efforts to bridge the gulf between science and art reached far beyond any "pseudo-scientific" search. By uniting two such fundamental, yet apparently disparate fields of inquiry and expression as science and art, Proust created a metaphorical bond that is as strong and pervasive as any scientific law. Despite his efforts, however, there are some minor mistakes in his scientific descriptions.

Proust was not a scientist, but his embracing outlook yielded a unified view of man and nature, the breadth of which has not been seen in the novel before or since. What is the definition of the scientific approach he used? Was he "modern" or "classical?" Can his work be seen as a watershed, containing both a classical, Cartesian, mathematical, rational, objective view, and a modern, subjective, intuitive attitude reflecting, in part, the emerging science of psychology? Can Proust's novel even be regarded as "post-modern," suggesting developments in psychology and physics not directly connected to his life, but which can be said to be part of the spirit of the time and is reflected in *In Search of Lost Time*?

What is the relevance of a particular science to Proust's novel—perspective, style, imagery, characterization—and how does it work? For Proust scholar Roger Shattuck, it is "principally through the science and art of optics that he beholds and depicts the world." Optics provides a vocabulary essential to Proust's thematic development. Not only does optics illuminate the external world, values, and development of the action, communicating these to the reader with a consistent vocabulary, but it also illuminates the inner world of the self. The optical imagery in *In Search of Lost Time* also affects the reader, allowing them to experience a sort of relativity resulting from the different perspectives of memory. These perspectives cause a change from a spatial to a temporal depth. As the normal subject-object relationship of reader to work dissolves, the book itself becomes a sort of optical instrument, as we shall see in a later chapter. The developments in glass include those in industry, science, art, and architecture. From *art nouveau* to aquariums, from the magic lantern to scientific instruments, glass can be considered an essential part of the structure of the novel.

For the Irish novelist Samuel Beckett (the subject of *Simply Beckett*), the majority of Proust's images are botanical. "He assimilates the human to the vegetal. He is conscious of humanity as flora, never as fauna." The imagery here is pervasive and describes Proust's "scientific" or "amoral" attitude toward people (which has upset more than one reader). Plants do not have free will, so cannot be judged. The "subjective" or internal world, as well as the state of the "objective" or external world is represented: "When the subject is exempt from will the object is exempt from causality (Time and Space taken together)." Out of this passive, plant-like state of self and its reflected relativistic world, the artist distills the essence of both. Proust participated here in both the German Romantic tradition, becoming *eins mit dem Weltall* (one with the world-all), and in the scientific tradition, probing the internal and external universe with a belief in a rationally verifiable order. This meeting of mystical, or Eastern, and scientific, or Western thought, is just one example of Proust's many striking achievements.

Medical sciences

The most frequently discussed of the scientific aspects is that of the importance of the medical sciences (in Proust's personal life, in his worldview, and in the imagery, language, philosophy, subject matter, and structure of his novel). Among the different medical sciences, that of the newly emerging science of psychology is perhaps the most important in *In Search of Lost Time*.

Though there is much discussion of what, if any, relationship there may have been between Proust's and Freud's views and their work, the opening of Charcot's clinic in Paris in 1880 appears to have played an important part in both their lives. Proust has also been compared to the Swiss psychiatrist Carl Jung; the two were interested in the unconscious mind. For the time being, however, let us simply note that Proust was not unique in his interest in the unconscious, but his psychological observations concerning man's subjective, internal universe, combined with his observations concerning physical laws of the "objective," external universe, are a very modern and unified view.

As with the physical certainties of time and space in the external world, the notion of an ordered, positivistic, fixed self also gives way to that of a more fragmented, relativistic plurality of selves. Parallels between Einstein's universe of physical laws and that of Proust's novel, itself made up of psychological laws, were made very early in its critical history. The mathematician Camille Vettard wrote a dedication in which he compared Proust to Einstein. The same Jacques Rivière, who boldly compared Proust to Sigmund Freud, rejected the dedication on behalf of the *Nouvelle Revue Française*. Vettard wrote a defense, in which he referred to Proust's style and ends, calling "M. Proust an Einstein of psychology or M. Einstein a Proust of physics." The world Proust has created reflects his own knowledge of both psychology and physics, the fundamental sciences in the effort to interpret nature and the psyche. Both Einstein and Proust have created worlds and, as William Carter pointed out, while Proust's creation is similar to that of Einstein's in its relativistic aspects, it also reflects the scientist's search for a Grand Unification Theory, or an underlying order which would tie together an otherwise fragmented and uncertain view of the world.

Scientific spectacles

The role of glass takes many forms–from the artistic to the scientific, and from the playful to all-embracing worldviews. Twice Proust referred to the work of Émile Gallé, one of the leading artists working with glass at the time. The first is in Balbec, in *Within a Budding Grove*. The Gallé-like images in the windows are a sort of superimposed display of Monet's water lilies and serve to separate the Narrator from the world. In the second reference, one can see the same elements–nature, a season, a moment captured in the glass of a window, and the Narrator's isolation.

It is through other objects of glass that the Narrator tries to break out of the glass cage of his room. The magic lantern, for example, recreates the young Narrator's bedroom. No longer is it an external light throwing an image on his window; rather, it is an internal projection, recreating the wall. The image of the magic lantern is a dominant one throughout the novel and can be seen as a symbol of the working of the imagination of the artist, projecting his vision onto the world and thereby recreating it.

Two other developments in the glass industry also serve to help the Narrator to explore the limits of the universe—from the smallest, using the microscope, to the vastest, using the telescope. The improvements in the quality of lenses played an important role in the expanding use of the microscope in the medical sciences, allowing increasingly precise observations in such fields as that of Proust's father, the epidemiologist Adrien Proust. The same improvements added to the ability to make still larger and more regular lenses, which helped expand the astronomer's vision outward. Proust's contemporaries envied the novelty and expanse of such an ability, and Proust made excellent use of it in his novel. His microscopic vision was only equaled by his use of telescopic or astronomical view, as seen in *Time Regained*, where his particular, microscopic descriptions are turned outward into an all-embracing, macrocosmic view of the universe.

Unlike the magic lantern, neither the telescope nor the microscope actually appear as part of the novel's décor. Instead, they are often used as metaphors, and serve to symbolize the "Proustian vision"—a search for an order, reaching from the most particular finite limits to the outermost limits of the visible universe, both expanded by contemporary developments in glassmaking. The microcosm reflects the macrocosm, and the world in the lens of the microscope displays traits and reveals an order similar to those found in the lens of the telescope. No wonder, then, that people should confuse the two. The Narrator's apprehension concerning the reception of his novel is founded on just this confusion of microscopic and telescopic views in time and space.

At the Guermantes' final party in *Time Regained*, where the Narrator is looking at the other members of the party "with the satisfaction of a zoologist," he sees some people who appear not to have aged. But if one looks closer, their faces look completely different, as they would if they were put under a microscope. A microscopic perspective in space provides the Narrator with a telescopic view in time. The result is another darkly funny passage where the Narrator is anything but omniscient.

Still another object of glass is taken out of Proust's world to be used in his novel. From 1850 to 1860, naturalists had rediscovered the aquarium as a means to reproduce the environment of aquatic creatures. Like the other objects of glass, the aquarium serves first as an instrument of observation, and then as an image of separation and confinement.

The subject-object relationship is still that of observer and observed, and the image of the aquarium allows the Narrator, like the scientists and their objects of study, to place the human species in a sort of laboratory-like atmosphere. The observer (the subject) is able to resolve the paradox of how to perceive a closed world. Human beings (the objects of the study) are allowed to continue in their natural routines and in their natural habitat, often unaware of any observers, as fish are unaware of people outside the aquarium (unless it is touched). Also, the object of study, the human race, has become just that—an object of study. The best example of that occurs at Balbec. The large bay window of the restaurant offers the Narrator his first view of many characters, including Albertine, Andrée, and Robert de Saint-Loup. Here the Narrator is part of the enclosed world of the "aquarium" (though it could be argued that, in the following description, the Narrator is the writer outside, looking in). The alienation here is not that of an individual, but of social classes: the elite of the "aquarium," dining in the restaurant of the Grand Hôtel, and the "others," the workers and the "petits bourgeois" outside the restaurant looking in. The effect is heightened with another contemporary development, electric lighting:

> hidden springs of electricity flooding the great dining-room with light, it became as it were an immense and wonderful aquarium against whose glass wall the working population

A Search for Certainty | 57

of Balbec, the fishermen and also the tradesmen's families, clustering invisibly in the outer darkness, pressed their faces to watch the luxurious life of its occupants gently floating upon the golden eddies within, a thing as extraordinary to the poor as the life of strange fishes or molluscs (an important social question, this: whether the glass wall will always protect the banquets of these weird and wonderful creatures, or whether the obscure folk who watch them hungrily out of the night will not break in some day to gather them from the aquarium and devour them).

The perspective is that of a "fish-eye" view, with the observed observing the observer observing him:

Meanwhile, perhaps, amid the dumbfounded stationary crowd out there in the dark, there may have been some writer, some student of human ichthyology, who, as he watched the jaws of old feminine monstrosities close over a mouthful of submerged food, was amusing himself by classifying them by race, by innate characteristics, as well as those acquired characteristics which bring it about that an old Serbian lady whose buccal appendage is that of a great sea-fish, because from her earliest years she has moved in the fresh waters of the Faubourg Saint-Germain, eats her salad for all the world like a La Rochefoucauld.

Besides the biting humor, the social question raised shows an awareness of the fragility of any social and economic hierarchy. This is only one example among many that repudiates the reputation for snobbery, social climbing, and worship of the rich and aristocratic that plagued Proust from his early pursuits and publications. One can also see a suggestion (albeit humorous) of the question of evolution, of inherited versus acquired characteristics.

Proust used the aquarium again as an image for the aristocratic Baron de Charlus and his own separation caused by social differences and sexual orientation. Unlike the Narrator, he is as much in touch with the opinions of the other members of the bourgeois Verdurin clan concerning himself as a fish is aware of people observing it in an aquarium. The Narrator, with his multiple perspectives, is conscious of his situation and can draw a comic conclusion. Charlus, however, is unaware of his precarious position in the Verdurin clan, or aquarium, and can only be pitied.

The last ocular instrument, the kaleidoscope, does not belong in the realm of science. The kaleidoscope is, in fact, the very antithesis of the common conception of a scientific instrument as cold, objective, precise, and analytical. It is a toy. It is a plaything with no practical purpose, amusing children and adults from the 19th century to the present day. Its "peephole" into "diverse and enclosed worlds" opens up, at the twist of a hand, a whole new order and a whole new world. It is not surprising that Proust used it as a very striking image of his own worldview, ever turning in the space-time continuum.

The Narrator's "perfect escape"

Unlike any of the other ocular images discussed so far, the telescope depends on nothing external to the instrument except light. It holds its own object of observation, not even requiring a blank wall onto which it must project its image. It is a perfect escape for the confined, the solitary, the uncertain Narrator. It is a perfect metaphor for a world in motion. The image appears early, in the third paragraph of *Swann's Way*, and is used to suggest the Narrator's semi-conscious state, one part awake, one part asleep. It is interesting to note that light–the only thing the kaleidoscope depends on–is absent. It is the light of consciousness that will try to fix this world in motion and the "kaleidoscope of obscurity" that surrounds the Narrator.

As with other instruments, it is also applied to society, which puts together different elements that one would have thought unapproachable. The kaleidoscope provides an image for the individual's relationship to society and a world in flux. But all these changes, the Narrator comments, do not keep people from thinking there will be no more changes. It also suggests Proust's notions of love and the contrast between the eternal verities of art and the ethereal judgments of the critical world. With the former, the kaleidoscope recalls the "kaleidoscope of obscurity." Now the Narrator is not only confused about the nature of things around him, but he is also in pain due to uncertainty with regard to people. "We think we know things exactly, and what people think, for the simple reason that we don't suspect anything. But as soon as we have the desire to know, like a jealous person, then it is a vertiginous kaleidoscope where we no longer distinguish anything."

Telescopes, microscopes, magic lanterns, windows, aquariums, and kaleidoscopes. All instruments of glass, and all undergoing fundamental changes in Proust's time. Each serves first as an instrument of observation, probing ever farther into space–both micro- and macrocosmic. Proust utilized each of the objects to observe not only in space, but also in time. He used the images of the instruments to describe his research into nature and the human psyche. While nearly all can be said to be "scientific"–involved in the rational, conscious, orderly collection through objective observation of classifiable data referring to a fixed world–they consistently point out the limits of such perceptual knowledge. Each instrument, while allowing closer observation, only serves to illuminate the Narrator's isolation and confinement. Only in art can they be escaped–art that is based on intuition, the antithesis of scientific activity. East meets West. The scientist Proust and the artist Proust, both exploring the worlds of nature and the psyche, are searching for laws, for order, for certainty. How better to begin the expression of his vision of the world than with optical theory?

7. Transportation

Even while confined, the importance of travel does not diminish for the Narrator. It only requires a different means of locomotion. Reading is the first of these immobile means of transport. The Narrator can slip out of his world and into the world of the work he is reading. He even leaves his own self, something that rarely, if ever, happens in physical travel. The chair he reads (and falls asleep) in becomes a magic chair. Sleep, the nightly (or daily) vertical voyage into the unconscious, is the second immobile means of escape. The Narrator compares it to traveling in an automobile, a train, and an airplane. Those uncertain moments of waking, already described as kaleidoscopic, are also compared to the experience of stepping off a moving train.

A similar experience of waking, not being able to anchor oneself in the surrounding world, with not only uncertainty regarding time and space, but also identity, is described in one of the Narrator's (and Proust's) favorite books, *The Arabian Nights*. "The Story of the Wakened Sleeper" is specifically mentioned in *Within a Budding Grove* when the Narrator, eating some cakes served on a plate, is reminded of his aunt's china at Combray which had pictures of *Aladdin* and his magic lamp, *Ali Baba*, *Sinbad the Sailor*, or *The Awakened Sleeper*. Like the Narrator, the protagonist, Abou Hassan is "in search of lost time"–in this case, the time he has lost being a good and prudent son. When his father dies, he parties away his inheritance, losing all the "friends" who came to enjoy his generosity. At the same time, the Calif Haroun-Al-Rashid leaves his palace for one of his nocturnal trips into the city. Disguised as a merchant, the Calif hopes to learn the undistorted truth of what is happening in the city, without letting anyone know it is the Calif who is wandering, observing. Proust provided both the Narrator and Charlus with the Calif's reasons for their own nocturnal prowling, adding another parallel with this Persian tale.

Coincidentally, Abou runs into the Calif and makes what he has decided will be his last invitation—he invites the stranger, for one night only, to come to drink, dine, and converse with him. Abou tells his story, expressing at the same time his wish to be Calif for a day. The Calif likes Abou, and allows him to realize this desire. He drugs him and takes him to the palace, ordering his servants to treat Abou as if he were the Calif. Abou wakes, confused by the things and people around him. The unfamiliarity of his surroundings and the uncertainty as to his own identity is that of the Narrator in the first pages of *Swann's Way*. The unreliability of the sort of memory—a willed, conscious effort to orient oneself—is similar in both stories.

The references to *The Arabian Nights* add a sense of mystery and magic to Proust's novel. They occur where there is some sort of displacement, traveling by an immobile or mobile means of transport. The story to which the Narrator refers most often, *The Story of the Awakened Sleeper*, while full of mystery and adventure, contains no magic at all. It is a chance encounter with the Calif that brings about the dramatic and confusing changes in Abou's life and identity. Coincidence replaces magic in this tale.

Like reading, sleep, and memory, drugs offer a magical means of immobile transportation in both Proust's world and the world of his novel. As an automobile can speed up or slow down, with the resulting alteration in the vision one has of the world passing by, so drugs may slow down or speed up the body with an equally altered world view. The Narrator's relationship with drugs is much the same as Proust's. It is clear that the Narrator is arguing from experience when he declares that the most powerful hypnotic is sleep itself and the effects of sleep are best known by someone who knows its absence. The Narrator is an expert, a collector of various types of sleep. In changing the time or place where he sleeps or in trying different drugs, the scientist is able to observe different types of sleep on his only possible subject, his own self. To this 'gardener of dreams,' the beauty he sees in variety is only surpassed by the beauty and strangeness of a sleep undistorted by drugs.

Finally, before turning to the Narrator's mobile means of

transportation, the invention and use of the telephone resulted in a dramatic change in civilization and Proust was aware of its importance. It was a new instrument and shook the old, habitual, limiting notions of fixed time, space, and self. Like a character from a magical tale, the Narrator can accomplish his miracle with the "magic receiver" of the telephone. He is amazed that through this "magic receiver," he can hear the disembodied voice of someone who is in a different place, perhaps even at a different time. Magic, far from being opposed to technology, is once again to be found in its advances. The combination offers one of the many comic episodes based on the Narrator's experiences. In a rising crescendo of worship of the telephone operators who oversee this mythological instrument, in one sentence he compares them first to "Vigilant Virgins," then "Guardian Angels," then "The All-Powerful," then the "Danaids of the Invisible." Finally, he refers to them as "ironic Furies" the "always irritable servants of Mystery, the shadowy priestesses of the Invisible, The Young Ladies of the Telephone" who cruelly interrupt an intimate conversation. But to have electricity and a telephone was a sign of modernity and part of the avant-garde. Of course, the Verdurins are among the first to have both. In contrast, others would have nothing to do with the mysterious object. Françoise refuses to answer the phone, so it is put in the Narrator's room. Even with it there, he fears missing Albertine's call, resulting in an immobility that forces the Narrator back into a direct rapport with the world around him, which once again is the enclosed realm of his room. He is aware of the slightest sounds, including the ticking of the clock.

 As with the ocular images, the telephone is first an instrument that helps the Narrator break out of the confines of his cage. It is a sort of conducting wire, uniting people over space and time. For the Narrator, it should be a welcome refinement of his system of communication with his grandmother at Balbec, where they tapped on the wall separating their adjacent rooms. On the contrary, due to the novel effect of hearing a disembodied voice, the Narrator hears her as never before, revealing her frailty and underscoring the isolation he feels when separated from his beloved grandmother.

Immobile means of transportation

The image of the train is introduced in the first paragraph of the first volume of *In Search of Lost Time*. Wondering what time it is when he wakes, the Narrator hears the whistle of trains, and is reminded of distances where a traveler is hurrying to the next station. The essential theme of memory is introduced, with the tracks of the train being engraved in the traveler's memory due to the excitement that comes from experiencing new places and unaccustomed acts inherent to travel, along with the enjoyment of returning to the place and people left behind. The fundamental opposition between novelty and habit that re-occurs throughout the novel is also introduced in the first moments of the always new and exciting trip that is *In Search of Lost Time*.

Trains are used both metaphorically and as one of the many "little enclosed worlds." In Chapter 3 of *Sodom and Gomorrah*, the Narrator recalls a particular trip along the coast of Normandy. The train offered Proust a chance to use another of the "little enclosed worlds"–the smallest being the compartment, then the corridor, then the train itself. There are occasional interruptions by such stations as Doncières, Grattement, Maineville, etc., which seem more like images in a magic lantern show, offering topics of conversation rather than a world with a reality external to that of the little world of the compartment. The spatial and temporal chain with the outside world has been broken. They have no idea where they are or what time it is.

While the aquarium in the restaurant of the Grand Hôtel at Balbec represented the "little enclosed world" for Proust, open to an ichthyologist's inspection, the train is more of a social chemist's test-tube. The compartment is poorly lit, allowing the Narrator to position himself in such a way that he can both imprison and take advantage of Albertine. The social chemistry begins heating up between the Narrator and Albertine. It cools briefly as he feels his chains to Albertine breaking by the experience of the freedom of travel. The train ride reawakens in him the desire to travel, to lead a new life, and finally to break up with Albertine.

A discussion of etymology provides the base for these acidic undercurrents. Proust's biting humor is apparent as Charlus joins the conversation between the other members of the compartment that include the pedant Brichot, the doctor Cottard, and the sculptor Ski. Charlus is obviously the object of Proust's acidic wit, but so are the Narrator and the three representatives of their professions in the "little world" in the little train. Charlus, a homosexual, asks for an explanation of the town name Thorpehomme, as he understands "homme" (meaning "man"), and this prompts the pedant to exchange knowing and malicious looks with the doctor and the sculptor. Brichot identifies the original Norse meaning of "homme" as "small island" and goes on to explain that another name, Orgeville, derives from the man's name, Otger (and therefore has nothing to do with "orge," meaning "barley"). Brichot's knowledge has the same effect on Charlus's "tendency" as it has on the Narrator's sense of mystery in names, the former losing the sex, the latter, the plant that makes up the second half (it actually means port). In both cases, the subjective projection onto the meaning of the word is lost, and the name of the place loses its particular significance. This is an especially disagreeable experience in Proust's eyes. A name is both an individual and a local thing. It is a name of a place, a person, and a family. It is a topological entity resulting from its physical as well as mental dimensions.

Another social (not to mention, sexual and comic) dimension is introduced at Doncières, where Robert de Saint-Loup is garrisoned and will often board the train with the other soldiers. Charlus's feigned concern over all the soldiers boarding the train is mocked as the Narrator holds Albertine prisoner with his look, as one of Robert's friends comes to deliver a message to the Narrator. Already submerged in the world of the compartment, the Narrator is almost fished out by another friend, Bloch, who wants him to meet his father, waiting on the bridge. But the Narrator, in an equally sad comment on the force of friendship in the face of love (and jealousy), cannot leave to do this simple gesture for fear of losing sight of Albertine, who might have messed around with Robert in his absence. He is as much a prisoner as she is, and his relationship with both friends suffers as a result. The whistling of the train (in contrast to the "sweet return home" it signifies at the very beginning of the novel) suggests the transience of friendship.

The chemistry and the humor heat up as Bloch is added to the compartment's mixture, causing a reaction in Charlus. So we see the Narrator in a frustrated effort to guard over Albertine. While watching out for Saint-Loup, he is talking to Bloch, who is trying to get the Narrator to leave the train to meet his father and who, in turn, has attracted Charlus's attention (who is pestering the Narrator with questions, trying to get to know Bloch). Ultimately, it is the Narrator who is in the comical position.

The train, then, is a series of enclosed worlds, opening onto the external world at different stops, as if they were scenes of daily life, framed in a picture. The trajectory of the train suggests novelty, the changes in life, the passing of time and space. It is both a positive suggestion, representing travel (both in the world and in the "countryside of the self") and a negative one, suggesting the transience of the world, the jealous, sado-masochistic relationships, the dissimulation and uncertainty inherent in society. However, it is the experience of riding in an automobile that truly captures Proust's imagination.

The change from the use of carriages to the ever-more common use of automobiles in Proust's lifetime is reflected in a passage found at the end of *Swann's Way* at the Bois de Boulogne. The Narrator is forced to face not only the reality of the passing of time, but also of place. They are both thin, unconnected, juxtaposed, and irretrievable slices. First, he is horrified and unaccepting, then defeated and suffering. Earlier in *Swann's Way*, however, the effects of riding in a car and the speed that it brings are presented. Due to the point in the narrative at which the young Narrator experiences it, Proust had to change the automobile to a speeding carriage. In an article he wrote for *Le Figaro*, entitled "Impressions on Riding in an Automobile" ("Impressions de route en automobile") he used his experiences with Agostinelli during a drive to Caen. He managed to keep something approximating the speed of a car while respecting the chronology of his story. The steeples he observed with Agostinelli become the steeples of Martinville and Vieuxvicq in the novel. The article is used with only a few other minor changes to provide what the Narrator wrote while speeding along in the carriage. It is the first realization of the Narrator's desire to be a writer as he translates his exhilaration into words on a page.

Words–the foundation of art as expressed through language–are the tools that will break the Narrator out of his confinement in time, space, and self, and in which he will find a new certainty, a new order, a new world view. The sense of mystery and of freedom in a name, a word, that the pedant Brichot destroyed in his etymological discussions held during the train ride described earlier, is reborn here, in this artistic flight. From the loss of the mystery in a name on the train, to an exploration in the place with the automobile, with a similar loss in mystery and meaning, to an unexpected experience in the place that will engender a new mystery and a new meaning, expressed in the word–which can be anything from the young Narrator's "Darn" to the piece given in the description of the steeples, to the entire work itself. Though meaning is not to be found in the place, it is only through a novel experience in the place that this new certainty can be born. It is not surprising then, that the place, the thing (here, the steeples), seem to contain and hide the new meaning.

The steeples

The Narrator has wanted to be a writer for a long time, waiting until he finds a subject of "infinite philosophical meaning" before he begins. This conscious effort of intellect will lead the Narrator nowhere, making him think he must have a physical or mental deficiency. Proust's black humor is evident as the Narrator concludes that, since he wants to be a writer, it is time that he decides what he is going to write about. But each time he tries, he only sees emptiness and thinks he might have a brain disease that keeps him from finding the topic. He had hoped that there would be help from above; from one of the accepted authorities of God, country, and family that would make him the greatest writer of his time. With the expected failure of these ironic appeals to an external authority, he renounces literature forever and accepts his own earthbound, limited existence; a boring life with no meaning, no magic. It seems that he is like any other person who will get old and die. The Narrator's search for certainty has apparently failed. Life has no meaning, no order, no certainty.

Then, unexpectedly, Marcel encounters the steeples, objects lacking in any abstract significance for him. In this experience, the Narrator finds meaning, pleasure, and power. Though rejecting the external authority and certainty found in a God, it is through his symbolic, material manifestation on earth, the steeples of Martinville and Vieuxvicq, that the Narrator will experience a new certainty, a new order, a new unity, coming from the depths of the self. The 'help from above' is actually a 'help from below.' There is Grace, but there is no God.

Bound in his physical and mental limitations, fixed in a dull world of habit and order, the Narrator's experience with the steeples is novel in a number of ways. Novelty is apparent in that the families' walk had been prolonged far beyond its normal duration. The speed of Dr. Percepied's carriage is increased to a speed normally not experienced. The Narrator's experience of a "special pleasure" comes about unexpectedly and suddenly at a curve in the road. The privileged moment of the "special pleasure" is outside the contingencies of a world fixed in habit, with reason and an external order based on particular objects grounded in particular places, at particular times. The notion of place is altered. The principle of causality is also in question as he experiences the "special pleasure" and, as in his experience with the tasting of the madeleine and herbal tea, he is frustrated at not knowing its origin.

He writes for the first time and, as the little piece is included, a geometric subject of "infinite philosophical meaning" is created in the form of a perspective to the infinite, suggested by the Chinese box-like effect of a work inside a work. In the piece, the Narrator describes the steeples of Martinville and Vieuxvicq as stark verticals on a horizontal plane. They are in motion. Minutes pass and, as the carriage speeds along, the steeples seem like three birds, posing immobile and outlined in the sun. The effect of relativity can be seen in the change in lighting, caused by the setting sun, the speed of the doctor's carriage, and in the changing perspective, caused by the winding road. As he approaches the steeples, in the light of the setting sun, they are like birds. A little later, looking back, with night falling, they are like three flowers, or three girls. Monet's paintings of different Rouen Cathedrals, transformed by the change in light at different times of the day, shows a similar transubstantiation of (religious) buildings. Hanging next to each other at the Musée d'Orsay, the paintings of the different-but-same cathedral reflect in a pictorial way part of what Proust was describing.

The importance of this passage cannot be overemphasized. The Narrator has written for the first time. His life has an original, individual meaning. His work has the "infinite philosophical meaning" he felt lacking. From stasis to motion, habit to novelty, boredom to adventure, death to life, the Narrator has filled in the "black hole," the "void" he faced earlier when trying to find something to write about. It is as if he has replaced a linear, strobe-like lens with a circular one, providing him with a revolutionary change in his world view, and freeing him from the confining limits of the contingencies of the mechanistic view of time and space.

Combray, previously only an isolated memory, a thin slice in time and space, is now seen in the round, as if arriving by train. In the experience with the carriage (or automobile) and steeples, another perspective to the infinite is added to this circular vision. It, too, is of a geometric nature. The Narrator has begun the resurrection of Combray through a chance encounter with an external object, the steeples of Martinville and Vieuxvicq. As he approaches the steeples, they are pointed up, a raised finger directing the way to God. However, the help and the grace that the Narrator experiences come not from an external force above, but from an internal one, from down in the depths of the self. Emptied of its religious meaning, unfixed in the ordered, empirical, mechanistic universe by the unsettling experience of relativity, the "finger" metaphorically falls, pointing now towards "the obscure landscape of the self." The external, physical world has been left for the internal, metaphysical world of the self, which Proust expressed so succinctly in one of his shorter, alexandrine-like sentences when he tasted the madeleine and tea: "I put down the cup and examine my own mind." The science of physics, with its order, its methodology, and its fixed laws has been left for the science of psychology, where the usual tools of the scientific trade must be abandoned: "It alone can discover the truth. But how? What an abyss of uncertainty, whenever the mind feels overtaken by itself: whenever it, the seeker, is at the same time the dark region through which it must go seeking and where all its equipment will avail it nothing. Seek? More than that: create."

The "meaning of infinite significance"

Proust recognized the inherent difficulty in this division of the self into observer and observed, rejecting the dualistic Cartesian maxim "I think therefore I am." He knew the experience to be real, though he did not know its cause, nor did it follow the rules of the mechanistic world. The experience is immediate, outside the contingencies of time, space, and logic. Thus, the privileged moment, the "special pleasure" offers a third possible "meaning of infinite significance," taking one out of the external, physical realm and into the countryside of the self—a world with a different set of laws unfettered by the confining and isolating cords of a positivistic worldview of time and space. It is the ultimate voyage next to death.

To return to the second possible "meaning of infinite significance"—if one looks at the intermediary movement, between the secured, upwardly and outwardly directed "finger of God" and its inversion downward and inward into the world of the self—one can see the first half of another circle being drawn by the falling finger. First, it is pointed up to God, life, light (the sun, the day), the external infinite, and creation. Then, unsettled in the experience of speed with its effects of relativity, the steeple metaphorically falls to the horizontal, pointing to the finite, physical world, made up of the contingencies of time and space. It is through the world of the senses, and through a chance contact with one of the particulars of reality that make it up, that the Narrator is thrown into the landscape of the self. The images of the steeples as three flowers and then as three girls serve to reinforce this sensual aspect. The "finger" is now pointed down, toward the infinite of the self, darkness (night), Satan, and death. The movement, however, does not stop here, for the artist must return to the world, recreating it with his new vision in a work of art. The "finger" has returned to the horizontal again, but it is not pointing to the same world. Rather, it is pointed to one recreated under the projection of the imagination of the artist. In this creative flight (reinforced by the images of the steeples as birds), the "finger" returns to the vertical, pointing to a new god, a new life, a new creation. The lines of the steeples have made a complete circle. His vision of Combray changed from that of a little slice to that of a circle. The geometrical design suggested by this movement is replicated in Proust's novel in a progression from the particular to the general: from the little madeleine (the lines of its scalloped bottom, the circle of its expansive top) to the novel itself (linear, in the sense that it is the life and times of the Narrator, and circular in that it ends where it began).

WWI and the airplane

In *Sodom and Gomorrah*, the Narrator is horse-back riding when he encounters more novelty and surprise than he expected in this already unaccustomed act when he hears what will be his first airplane. He describes the pilot as a mythological demi-god who seems to break even the law of gravity. According to Proust's young friend at the seaside retreat, Marcel Plantevignes, it was his own equestrian experience at Cabourg that inspired the writer, but Proust was already interested in this important development, affecting not only man's life, but also his worldview. The beauty and exhilaration of the feeling of flight also had an undeniable appeal to Proust and is reflected in his novel. The incident is a precursor to the highly apocalyptic passage surrounding the incident in Jupien's male brothel, where confusion has hit an entire city and the plane has become a squadron bringing death. In *Time Regained*, airplanes are introduced on a large scale. World War I and the darkness of the night are augmented by the blackout of the city lights. The advent of war has precipitated the use of the airplane. Proust was not only conscious of the beauty and death it represents, but he was also conscious of its intrusion into the one area of apparent stability and unchanging order to which man had looked since the times of the Babylonians: the stars. Speaking to Robert de Saint-Loup, the Narrator describes the planes as becoming part of the constellations, obeying human laws that are as precise as those of the immutable stars. With their movement, they break the laws of the celestial clockwork and disrupt the previously unchanging order of the cosmos. The Greek god described earlier in the novel is now seen more in the Germanic tradition with Wagnerian overtones.

It is here, in wartime Paris, where the Narrator follows Charlus into Jupien's male brothel, that Proust showed some of his darkest humor. After showing the universality of homosexuality in the diversity of the clientele, the Narrator describes an encounter between Jupien and a priest who tries to leave without paying. Raising a "finger of a doctor in theology," the priest excuses himself, saying he is not "an angel." After having apologized for his unorthodox and–according to the teaching of the church–immoral behavior, the priest tries to break even the one law of Jupien's establishment: he tries to slip out without paying his bill. Never missing a beat, Jupien, like his religious counterpart, asks for his contribution to help with "the expenses of the cult" before leaving. The priest painted by Proust is clearly outshined in wit and honesty by the owner of the male brothel. Jupien speaks the Narrator's language when he responds to the latter's reference to *The Arabian Nights* with one of his own. The interplay between imagination and reality (from the images of the magic lantern to the "sexual hell" seen through a peephole to the allusions to *The Arabian Nights*) is further compounded by Jupien's reference to John Ruskin's *Sésame et les Lys* that the Narrator had sent to Charlus. Jupien's little enclosed world is his magical domain, open only on his command, as in the story of "Ali-Baba and the Forty Thieves."

Moving outward, away from his room, the Narrator encounters novelty in a series of sensorial contacts with the particulars of a very ordinary reality–the smell of the varnish of the stairway leading from his room to downstairs, the taste of the madeleine and herbal tea in the living room, the sight of the light on the lines of the steeples of Martinville and Vieuxvicq–all of which provide him with the extraordinary experience necessary for the creation of the memories that will make up his immense edifice. In the movement outward, one sees another aspect in this search for certainty, that is, with these sensorial contacts, the Narrator is sure that what he experiences is the real, external world and not simply a projection of his own imagination, like that of the magic lantern onto the wall of his childhood room. He must prove that it has body, that it is not simply a play of light, but also has a physical, objective reality.

8. Proust and the Human Sciences

In *In Search of Lost Time*, the Narrator's quest for certainty in the external world leads him repeatedly back to the individual. The Narrator's efforts to understand the laws of the immediate physical world and, reaching even farther out of the celestial mechanics, cause further uncertainty. The order he hopes to find in the objective, empirical world is inextricably bound to the subject doing the searching. To find meaning, therefore, one must understand both the world and man.

    The Narrator looks at man both as species and as individual. He considers him as a physical being, manifesting laws in the objective world, and also as a metaphysical or spiritual being, manifesting laws in the subjective world. In so doing, the scientist, looking for empirical laws in an objective universe, using his intellect and reason, must join with the artist who, using intuition, follows a different methodology in his own search in man's internal landscape. A "grave uncertainty" experienced by the Narrator while experimenting with the madeleine and herbal tea grows from his realization of the need for a new methodology. He puts down the cup, turns to his self, and realizes that he needs new equipment in this quest where he is at the same time the one searching and the strange, obscure land that is being discovered, concluding that it is not only a question of searching but also of creating. So, while the Narrator considers man as a naturalist (a physical being obeying objective, verifiable laws), he will finally turn his vision to man's internal, subjective world, the domain of the psychologist and artist. It is there that he will finally find his certainty, his fixed essence in a relativistic world in flux.

Unacknowledged influence of Schopenhauer

One of the more famous of Proust's possible influences was a French philosopher, Henri Bergson. Aside from being related to Bergson by marriage (Bergson was married to Proust's cousin Louise Neuberger), some critics argue that Proust had read Bergson's writings and had even studied under him at the Sorbonne (although Bergson never held a post there). Others disagree. As early as November 12, 1913, in an interview with the newspaper Le Temps, Proust himself—while acknowledging a common interest—made a distinction between them. His novel should be considered a "series of novels of the Unconscious," rather than "Bergsonian" novels. While this in itself does not preclude parallels, convincing cases have been made supporting a Germanic influence on Proust, particularly through the ideas of the 19th-century German philosopher Arthur Schopenhauer. Proust's philosophy professor, Alphonse Darlu, was the likely source of this not-so-general knowledge. While studying theories of perception, dreams, memories, the self, the reality of the external world, and of space and time with Darlu, Proust began developing his theories. Many items often attributed to Bergson—including Proust's famous distinction between voluntary and involuntary memory—are derived from Schopenhauer.

But if Schopenhauer's influence was so strong and so direct, why did Proust not acknowledge it? He only mentioned the German philosopher twice in his novel (both times as a sign of Mme de Cambremer's intelligence). And though there are only three references to Schopenhauer in Proust's (published) correspondence, they suggest a familiarity with his philosophy. In 1905, he wrote to Mme de Noailles of Schopenhauer's theory concerning the unity of the world. The following year, he flattered Robert de Montesquiou with the expressed regret that his friend's letter, while more profound than Schopenhauer's theory, should be reserved for only himself alone. In 1911, he made a reference to Schopenhauer in a letter to the musician Reynaldo Hahn, with whom he often discussed musical theory. Nowhere, however, is there a clear acknowledgment of his debt to either the Germans in general or Schopenhauer in particular.

The answer lies, perhaps, with the French prejudices against the Germans. The Narrator speaks of Robert de Saint-Loup's unusual intelligence and independence of spirit, manifested in his many Germanic references, in the same way as he referred to Mme Cambremer. One simply did not speak of the Germans. While aware of contemporary German thought, the typical French pedant such as Brichot showed little sympathy for German influences, reflecting the general attitude of most of his countrymen regarding the role Germany played and the death and destruction experienced by France in World War I. In addition, because of the presumed difficulty of the language and the comfortable comparisons with Bergson, one can better understand perhaps why this particular influence has not been as fully discussed as it should have been.

Following family interest in medicine

The background of Proust's interest in medicine is particularly easy to trace. The influence of his father and brother cannot be ignored. Both were doctors. His father was one of the leading practitioners in France, establishing, in 1866, a *cordon sanitaire*—a kind of quarantine—against cholera. It has been suggested that the Spanish tour taken by the Narrator's father with the diplomat M. de Norpois in *In the Shadow of Young Girls in Flower* is based on the investigation of an outbreak of cholera led by Dr. Proust. Ironically, it was through his interest in pathology that Adrien Proust became involved in the newly emerging science of psychology. Of the different clinics developing in Paris during the 1880s, one (whose directors were Pierre Janet and Jean-Martin Charcot) was staffed with pathologists. Through Charcot's clinic, Dr. Proust became involved in the study of hypnotic sleep, and eventually took a patient's case ("Emile X") to the Académie des sciences morales. Janet believed that man's moral and physical existence is defined by both his healthy and his unhealthy attributes. To the artist, this offered a new, "scientific" methodology for his search in the human landscape. While the artists looked to the psychologists for a scientific methodology, the psychologists looked to the artists as rare subjects of observation in their own quest for the laws governing the internal countryside of man.

Proust's personal knowledge of the work being done by Charcot and the others was not limited to that gained through his father. He was also very close to the Daudet family, who themselves had ties with their neighbor, Charcot. Léon Daudet, who was studying to be a doctor at the time, was personally interested in this new shared ground between scientist and artist. Both medicine and literature are involved in observing human beings. The symbiotic relationship between psychologist and artist formed the foundation for a vision of the man's inner world as radically new, as were the innovations in the technical and physical sciences for man's vision of the world outside. Both also provided new tools to aid in the search for laws, and both end, paradoxically, in revolutionary world views. This may help to explain why, while some critics pointed to Proust's "new intellectual mysticism," others described him as a dispassionate observer and his observations, therefore, as scientific data. This is the inescapable paradox of any effort to objectively and scientifically observe the nature of man. How does one arrive at a rational explanation of the laws governing man's subjective nature, which is both objectively verifiable and predictable according to physical, causal, connecting principles? Is it possible to observe man's nature without distorting it—either by the subject's awareness of being observed, or by some moral interpretation on the part of the observer?

Aside from the particular influences of family, teachers, and friends, it should also be evident that Proust's psychological inquiries were not an aberration but, rather, a reflection of the spirit of the times. The possible Freudian influences seen by some critics in *In Search of Lost Time* are due not to any direct knowledge Proust might have had of the psychologist's work, but rather to their shared intellectual development that was prevalent among intellectuals in France at the end of the 19th century. Proust's timing could not have been better: Freud had received a grant to study with Charcot from 1885 to 1886. Proust shared Freud's belief in the existence of another unconscious self and the roles dreams and hypnosis play in revealing it.

Proust the pathologist

Adrien Proust's primary field of expertise manifests itself in his son's novel in a number of ways.

First, Marcel used precise pathological descriptions to suggest the inescapable passing of time and as a reflection of the unobservable, internal state of an individual. In *Time Regained*, the Narrator attempts to see the order, the law working behind the destruction he sees in the faces around him. A change in hair color completely alters a face that is nevertheless the same in structure. Another face impresses the Narrator by its immobility, suggesting "arteriosclerosis." The descriptions continue in a series of darkly humoristic encounters that remind the Narrator not only of the passing of time, but also of several practical medical observations that can seem to either speed it up or slow it down.

Proust also used his knowledge of pathology to describe the experience of love. Again, we see a major means of escape from the confines of the self cut off from the Narrator (and here, Swann). Love is not a means of liberation, a source of new meaning, or new certainty. Love is a disease (or, rather, a number of them). Though it is in the last few hundred pages of *In Search of Lost Time* that one finds the most references to medicine, specific references to love as a disease are to be found throughout the novel. Swann is in love like "a drug addict or a consumptive." He is not only sick, but he is also addicted to the point that there is little hope for his recovery. Even the most audacious surgeon would ask himself if removing the disease is possible. Swann admits to becoming neurotic. He hopes he will live long enough to ask Odette about an affair she may have had. But this, too, can only be another stage in the progression of his disease. One can never know the truth through another, above all from someone loved. Writing of the Narrator's love for Gilberte, Proust described the obstacles to truth as being like a tumor. The inability of anyone to understand someone else's love is similar to the astonishment people have when faced with a scientific fact, the cause of which is unobservable, such as a "comma bacillus" being the cause of cholera.

Jealousy is also described as a physical disease. It is like "tuberculosis" or "leukemia." Infidelity is as common as a cold, with everyone having their own way of falling sick. It is a complicated disease, as the source and the remedy are the same. The object of love is both a poison and an antidote. Finally, as is evident in the story of Swann's love for Odette, love is an incurable disease "like those diathetic states in which rheumatism affords the sufferer a brief respite only to be replaced by epileptiform headaches." In one of many succinct sentences, the Narrator explains that what he means "by love [is] reciprocal torture." The Narrator is freed, and the disease is partially excised with Albertine's death, but it is not until the passing of time has its effects that this "general disease called love" can be defeated by the "general law of oblivion." Time kills, but it also heals.

Pathology plays a major role in Proust's novel. Nearly all of his characters have some kind of disease. There remains one important character who is not defined by a disease: his mother. Yet the Narrator's love for his mother is defined, in essence, by the "goodnight kiss" denied the young Narrator at bedtime. This denial will dominate his life, becoming at least a part of the origin of his debilitating love for Albertine.

Throughout his life, the Narrator searches for the sense of

certainty lost in the denial of his mother's ritual bedtime kiss. Though well separated not only in time and space, but also in a very different moral and social world, the description of the Freudian scene is strikingly similar to that of Charlus in Jupien's male brothel near the end of the novel. Both places are sources of pain for the Narrator and Charlus, respectively. Both are closed, shut off from the world. In the scene with Charlus, the sense of imprisonment is enhanced by the necessity of keeping all the windows shut due to the wartime blackout. It is due in part to the stuffy air that the Narrator leaves room number 43 and observes Charlus chained to his iron bed. As for the young Narrator, even on the stairs leading to his room, smelling the odor of the varnish on the stairs, his experience is less than comforting. Once inside his room, the prison-like atmosphere is complete. All the exits are blocked, the shutters closed, and his own grave is dug. Even their beds are similar. First, the Narrator's: his iron bed that had been moved in because he was too hot in the other bed. Before going to bed, he feels like a condemned man. The parallel further points out the similarities between the two apparently different passages. The origins of Charlus's tendencies are not as easily distinguishable from other people's as one might think. His desire to be chained and beaten reveals a desire that is as poetic as other people's wish to travel. Because Charlus wanted this dream to be as real as possible, he had Jupien sell the wooden bed that was in room 43 and replace it with an iron one that went better with the chains. The magical voyage of sleep and dreams takes place in neither the Narrator's nor Charlus's iron bed.

   Thus, even the most innocent of childhood scenes and the purest of loves are homologous to the sexual hell of Jupien's house as described in *Time Regained*. As the reassuring certainty of the ritual bedtime kiss is replaced by the anguished uncertainty of his solitary bedroom exile, so is the poetic illusion of love succeeded by the paradoxical iron unreality of a threatening, sado-masochistic hell.

   Swann inhabits a similar inferno. Due to his love for Odette, he is "like a sick person ... in a new circle of hell from which he wasn't able to perceive how he would ever be able to escape."

Along with the Narrator, these three characters—Odette, Swann, and Charlus—represent Proust's search for laws in man's moral, sociological, and biological nature. As the object of Swann's secret, enslaving desire, Odette is an example of the impossibility of a certainty based on an everlasting, mutual love. In Charlus, one sees the search for natural and psychological laws, and in Swann, the quest for natural and sociological laws. The parallels made by Proust between the psychological patterns of homosexuals and the social position of Jews are well documented.

Before turning to Proust's search for naturalistic and psychological laws, one might ask why he chose members of two such seemingly unrepresentative "races" as subjects for his inquiries into the laws of man. Both are suspect, and both are judged. The former stands as a quintessential representative of universal sin, while the latter represents man's inevitable submission to racial laws.

Proust's choice of Charlus is in the tradition of Pierre Janet's previously cited belief in the importance of studying not only the healthy, but also the ailing man before he can be understood. In his inescapable need for dissimulation, Charlus is a microcosm of society in general. Though they must be hidden, his sexual obsessions exhibit one of the fundamental laws of nature itself. He is just another aspect of the same reality, representing "an admirable, unconscious effort of nature." His hidden side is out of the control of his will, his intelligence, and his reason, just as a plant is when it follows its basic natural laws. For some critics, Charlus is "too much" to accept. For others, he is quite real, and the only surprising thing is that there are not more homosexuals in Proust's novel.

The little enclosed world of Jupien's male brothel provides an ideal source of information concerning this hidden society. Because of the nature of Jupien's highly clandestine hotel, the Narrator is provided with an even greater satisfaction when its reality is revealed. It is so secretive as to be considered as possibly subversive, with its members being mistaken for spies. Seeing Charlus enter the brothel, even the Narrator is forced to ask himself if Jupien's hotel might be a meeting place for spies. Proust's interest in this society certainly may have other causes, but it is also consistent with Janet's philosophy and with Proust's overwhelming desire to penetrate the veil of perceived truth to arrive at the hidden reality. This is true of his relationship with the enclosed, separate, mysterious world of the aristocracy (represented here by the Baron de Charlus), as well as with the world of the working man, (represented by Jupien, a former employee of the Narrator's family and present owner and maître d'hôtel of the brothel). This penchant for mystery and its revelation was an essential part of Proust's (and the Narrator's) character and beliefs. Their enjoyment of such scenes is that of a naturalist describing a new discovery.

9. Proust the Naturalist

Proust's interest in the science of human natural history is evident throughout *In Search of Lost Time*. One only has to look at the title of the second volume, *Within a Budding Grove*, to see a general suggestion of the naturalistic direction Proust would follow in his search. The description of the Narrator's first sighting of the girls on the beach is assimilated to an insect's view of a plant (here, a geranium): different, seductive patterns perceived in a way not apparent to the normal human observer. This association of human natural science with that of insects, plants, and animals is fundamental to Proust's philosophy and his novel.

Proust was well aware of the groundbreaking work of the naturalist Charles Darwin (1809-1892) and Darwin may have provided the inspiration for these associations. The first specific reference to Darwin appears in the third volume, *The Guermantes Way*. Oriane (the Duchesse de Guermantes)—giving credit to Swann for her knowledge of botany—compares what goes on at night between humans in the *Bois de Boulogne* to what is happening in the corner of her garden in plain daylight: the latter differing only in its comparative simplicity of consummation. Her somewhat less knowledgeable cousin, who hasn't heard of Darwin, is unable to appreciate the subtleties of Oriane's comparisons when she replies that the commode where the plant is sitting is splendid also and that it is in the *Empire* style.

While the role of naturalism is apparent throughout the novel, it is in the fourth volume, *Sodom and Gomorrah*, that it truly flourishes. On the first page, with the description of a "natural" discovery, the Narrator's position is that of a botanist. He has placed himself in such a way as not to disturb any insect that might pollinate the duchess's plant. From his position, he is also able to observe another chance encounter, while remaining unobserved himself. Now, however, it is between two members of the human species: Charlus and Jupien. The stage is set for a naturalistic description of man heretofore not seen in any novel. According to the Narrator, "the laws of the vegetal world are governed by laws that are higher and higher." Naturalistic reflections such as this form an integral part of the novel and, if this is not already apparent to the reader, the Narrator makes it so when he declares he has "already drawn from the apparent ruse of flowers a conclusion concerning a whole unconscious part of the literary work."

The Narrator loses sight of the bee (Charlus) and—while wondering if Charlus is the bee intended by the orchid Jupien—he ponders the "providential chance" that brought these two together.

The scene appears to be so rooted in the natural sequence of the mating process that the Narrator imagines a series of naturalistic transformations, seeing "successively a man, a man-bird, a man-fish, a man-insect." In looking to animals and plants, Darwin hoped to discover the laws governing man's biological nature. Conversely, Proust—observing man—saw the predetermined playing out of the same laws that govern the lower orders. They shared a fundamental belief in the natural unity of all life.

The choice of a homosexual encounter to represent Darwin's theory of natural selection (which depends on those individuals best adapted for the reproductive success of their kind) is, to say the least, paradoxical. A possible explanation is that the survival of the species is not based on as simple a law as that described above. Discussing the psychological games going on between Morel and Charlus in *Time Regained*, the Narrator suggests that the homosexual relationship serves as a kind of Malthusian braking mechanism for the human race, thereby aiding in its ultimate survival.

This Malthusian interpretation of the paradox is evident on a larger scale in the description surrounding Marcel's visit to Jupien's male brothel. Here—in wartime Paris—the German airplanes become the insects, and Paris is the flower. The *a priori* restraining effects of the obviously non-reproductive homosexual act, as seen in Jupien's brothel, is equaled (if not eclipsed) by the *a posteriori* reduction in population incurred during war, witnessed here on the national or macrocosmic scale. Proust judged neither from a moral standpoint. Rather, they are described as a natural scientist might.

In his inquiry into the natural history of man, Proust also asked some fundamental questions concerning the laws governing the hereditary nature of man. The homosexual case offers a perfect vehicle for the (still unanswered) question concerning acquired versus inherited traits. Could this trait (homosexuality) be passed on from generation to generation and, if so, was it acquired at some point by an ancestor? Whether it is an innate or acquired trait is one of the fundamental questions that Proust addressed but did not resolve. Aside from any moral considerations, experimentation on humans would not be practical. The experiment would take generations to observe. Proust, therefore, could not have participated in an active way in the newly emerging, predominantly German and Austrian scientific activity of experimental biology. There is no question, however, that Proust shared this modern scientific attitude. His theories are based on observations made in his world, and they provide the raw data for the Narrator's similar thoughts and activities.

Hypothesizing and confining himself to natural history, the Narrator debates the shared traits of the Guermantes family. If, as seems possible, it is a "perverted family," then it is not members such as Charlus and Robert de Saint-Loup who show hereditary faults. Rather, it is the heterosexual Duc de Guermantes who is the exception. In his particular taste for men, Robert de Saint-Loup may be exhibiting an inclination, a trait inherited from some past relation who acquired a similar taste. His activities, then, would not be the result of choice (and therefore open to moral judgment), but of scientific necessity. And what role do chance and random mutation play in all this? Proust's interest in this subject was not an isolated case. From Einstein to Bergson, these matters were clearly part of the intellectual discussions of the time, intended to clarify man's relationship to the universe, where choice becomes necessity and causality's role is replaced by chance.

Proust the psychologist

Proust had defined *In Search of Lost Time* as an effort to create a "series of novels of the Unconscious." That Proust was not only considering man's internal landscape from a philosophical and metaphysical point of view, but also trying to elucidate psychological laws, is evident in his numerous and precise references in the novel. While listening to conversations during dinner, the Narrator is examining the mentalities which produced them, resulting in a pattern that reveals to him an "ensemble of psychological laws." It is the instinct of the artist that draws the general out of the particular and that hears in the insignificant babble of social parrots the "spokesperson of a psychological law." It is the "game of different psychological laws" that aids in the flowering of the human race.

It is true, however, that these precise references occur only in the final volume of Proust's novel, *Time Regained*. The term "unconscious" is not used until the third volume, *The Guermantes Way*, and the first correspondence does not happen until 1915. The evolution of Proust's thoughts concerning the nature of man's psyche can be seen in two references from his novel, one from the first volume and the other from the sixth, *The Fugitive*. In the first reference, taken from the end of "Combray" (the first section of *Swann's Way*), the Narrator's description of memory is purely spatial. He uses geological terms to represent the nature of the formation of memory, bringing to mind those used by Darwin in his description of the formation of atolls, which helped prove the age of the earth, giving strength to his theory of evolution. In *The Fugitive*, Proust introduced the role of the fourth dimension of time in his psychological description of memory and its partner, "oblivion."

The loss of a fixed frame of reference is as much internal as it is external. Not only is the order in the space-time continuum in flux, affecting the objective set of correlatives, but the subjective apparatus of the self, the single, indivisible, subject is also in doubt.

The self is seen now as a plurality of selves. This is due to two factors, one having to do with developments in psychology, the other related to changes in physics. It is a reflection of the psychological developments of the times, postulating the existence of an unconscious beneath the social masks worn by individuals. The existence of one or more "selves" beneath this façade was also prevalent among psychologists and other writers of the time.

   The plurality of selves is not only one of a sedimentary layering of levels of consciousness. The Platonic Ideal, having undergone an amoeba-like transformation with the Socratic "Know Thyself" (and, later, with René Descartes's dualistic splitting of man into subject and object, knower and known with his famous "I think, therefore I am") has become a futile attempt to arrest time. It is a slip-sliding plurality of selves based on memories associated with events taking place in the flux of the space-time continuum. The references to this particular plurality of selves abound in Proust's novel and vary from a single temporal division when the Narrator refers to "the self that we were" to an innumerable plurality of selves that make us who we are, where each self must undergo the pain of Albertine's departure.

   Memory itself is divided, as seen in Proust's well-known distinction between voluntary and involuntary memory. His distinction, while developed to a point unparalleled in literature, philosophy, or psychology, is not original and was being discussed at many venues, from literature to journals, to scholarly presentations. Once again, Proust's philosophical and psychological theories were in many respects reflections of the spirit of the times.

   As with the distinction between a conscious and an unconscious self, the division between voluntary and involuntary memory served to remove the subject from the contingencies of a Cartesian, reasoning, logical and linear self, placing it in an unconscious, instinctive, non-willed realm, presumably outside the bounds of time and space. But what exactly (if "exactness" is a term that can be applied in the field of psychology) is the nature of this unconscious? Is there a singular *Unconscious* (recalling Proust's reference to "The

Unconscious")—an indivisible, core Self "below" the slip-sliding uncertainty found in the plurality of selves closer to the surface of consciousness? Before answering these questions, however, it is important to examine how Proust proceeded in his search for this underlying essence. Before judging the value of his theory of the Self and of the Unconscious, his means of finding it must be considered. As always with Proust, it is not only the thing in itself, but also the process and the methodology used to arrive at it and the means to express it that provide the adventure of the quest.

10. Three Types of Observation

There are three types of observation in *In Search of Lost Time*, each reflecting a different relationship between the object of observation and the observer. Briefly, they can be described as separation, interaction, and fusion. In the first (separation), the post of observation is clearly defined. The observer is purely a spectator. In the second (interaction), the observer is involved with the observed, being drawn into the spectacle. In the third (fusion), there is no distinction between the observer and the observed, the spectator and the spectacle, the subject and the object. Difficulties are inherent to each type of observation and are shared by both Proust and psychologists in general. Proust's three types of observation also help answer the question of whether he was classical, modern, or post-modern, reflecting, as they do, the developments in the history of science of all three worldviews.

There are three striking examples of the first type of observation in Proust's novel. In order of occurrence, they are: when the Narrator observes Mlle. Vinteuil at her father's house in Montjouvain, as she and her girlfriend "celebrate" the death of her father; when the Narrator observes the encounter between Charlus and Jupien in the courtyard of the hotel de Guermantes; and when, having followed Charlus into Jupien's male brothel, the Narrator observes him chained to a bed. It should be of no surprise that, in each case, the Narrator is hidden from view and the participants have no idea that he is there. This point is made quite clear in each of the three cases. In Monjouvain, the Narrator is hidden in the shadows outside Mlle. Vinteuil's room. In the courtyard, he is hidden first on a stairway, and then behind a window whose shutters are only half shut. He listens, careful not to be discovered by Jupien or Charlus. In the brothel, he is able to watch Charlus thanks to a round window whose curtain someone forgot to shut, while remaining undetected in the shadows.

Voyeurism versus observation

While some see this as a manifestation of Proust's voyeuristic tendencies, others see here an example of his effort to develop a clear, scientific situation in which to observe the human species in its undisturbed activities. Not only is it important that the spectacle remain undisturbed, but the spectator must have a detached, classically scientific sense of objectivity. In each case, it is made clear that the Narrator (whatever the case may have been with Proust himself) is not present at the spectacle in order to satisfy any voyeuristic tendencies. He is also devoid of any moral prejudice towards or emotional involvement with the participants. At the Vinteuil house in Monjouvain, he finds himself in his unique position because he has fallen asleep. He stays there only out of fear of being detected. As already seen, the Narrator is in the courtyard of the hotel de Guermantes because of his botanical interests. While the motivation is slightly different here, and the Narrator's spying has become more purposeful, it is due only to a detached curiosity. By the time of the scene at Jupien's brothel, the Narrator's curiosity has emboldened him to an even more active effort in his spying when he climbs the stairs and puts his ear to the door. This more vigorous attitude, however, still does not show any personal involvement. It was only with a detached suspicion of espionage mixed with curiosity and thirst that the Narrator ever entered the establishment.

At the same time that one can see an increase in the Narrator's morally, emotionally, and sexually detached curiosity, one can also note a more penetrating movement with regard to the staging of the spectacle. In the first instance, he is outside the house, in the yard. In the second, he has moved into the enclosed space of the courtyard. In the third, he has entered the confines of a whole society, itself closed off from the world by Jupien's establishment; he is able to observe the spectacle of Charlus's masochism from a corridor outside the room. Even before he watches Charlus undetected, he is able to observe the other members of the society with the same dissimulation, that is, standing in the shadows. This sense of having crossed several barriers, which keep him from the truth, reflects his effort to penetrate the levels of conscious will in order to arrive at the hidden unconscious.

In all three of these scenes, Proust had taken care to keep the Narrator in the privileged position of a detached intellectual attitude and activity with regard to the study of the world. In Aristotle's time, the abstract noun "theoria" denoted the activity of spectating, observing any activity or process in contrast to intervening, participating, or being an agent. This was the predominant scientific attitude until, including and after the time of Descartes and Isaac Newton. Descartes not only divided mind from matter, but he also set man apart from nature and established "rational objectivity" that placed the scientist in the position of pure spectator.

As has been pointed out by philosophers of science, the notion of a scientist as a pure spectator is dead. The earlier ideal of rational objectivity confronting a causal, linear world is an illusion. A new method of inquiry of developing and expressing laws concerning both world and man is essential. While this is particularly true in psychology, where the object of observation is the human unconscious, it also relates to the world of physics. This is true, for example, in the often-used Heisenberg Principle, where, by the very act of observation, the particles being observed behave differently. This involvement of the spectator in the spectacle, with its inherent loss of a certainty based on reason, logic, and objectivity, is nowhere more apparent than in the Narrator's relationship with Albertine.

A "lesson in relativism"

The uncertainty of the Narrator, who is both observer and lover, combined with the uncertainty of the observed and the loved one—Albertine—caused the former to doubt the very existence of any causal principle at all. The relationship is a "lesson in relativism." Once involved in the spectacle, the observer, no longer detached, is firmly anchored to the object of observation and even one's being exists "only by what one possesses." Though every effort is made to imprison Albertine, she escapes. Like any person, she is not an object. She is an agent and, as such, is not subject to "objective" rules of verification. In the mechanistic worldview, the scientist is supposed to remain detached and objective, observing without being drawn into the event. First of all, the Narrator is drawn "into" Albertine. The requirement of a rational distancing is destroyed. Second, the object of observation is not an object, but a dynamic process. Third, both observer and observed are immersed in time and, as such, cannot have the fixed frame of reference necessary for information gathering, or even the same observer or observed, because, at the time of each event, there is a different Albertine and a different Narrator.

In the third type of observation, there is a fusion between subject and object, between observer and observed. In psychological terms, this is referred to as self- or auto analysis. Having realized the difficulties inherent in any study of the nature of man's unconscious from an external position, from outside the self of an "other," the only recourse left in Proust's endeavor is to look inside himself.

Freud, reaching the same conclusion, soon realized that true self-analysis is not possible either.

The first instance of fusing of subject and object occurs in Proust's novel when the Narrator tastes the madeleine and herbal tea. While aware that some internal essence is making itself known, the Narrator is also conscious of the difficulties inherent in any research he might employ in order to discover its nature. He tastes the mixture. A "delicious pleasure" has invaded him, without any idea as to its cause. He asks himself where it came from, what it means, and how to seize it? He takes a few more mouthfuls and realizes this "delicious pleasure" lies in himself. He puts down the cup and turns to his "esprit" or mind. The search for the truth is now in its hands. But how should he go about it? It is not only a question of looking, but also of creating. Freud reached a similar conclusion. The self is like a slide in a magic lantern. By looking at its projection in a work of art (here, the written word), one can study the nature of the unconscious that produced it. This free expression of the unconscious requires a temporary setting aside of conscious will and intellect. No encounter is willed. Each comes about by chance. Each experience forms a part of involuntary memory. What involuntary memory was for Proust, free association was for Freud.

The nature of the unconscious and vision of the world

It is here that we begin to arrive at the nature of the unconscious. A work of art—in particular a metaphor—unites an internal, subjective truth of the self with an external, "objective" truth of the world. The unity is not imposed; it comes from inspiration and not from "the artificial development of a thesis." In the encounter with the steeples of Martinville and Vieuxvicq, where the Narrator wrote for the first time, an unexpected sensation, aroused by an unplanned perception of a particular object, results in the creation of a work of art. But, as the Narrator points out later in the novel, any knowledge we have is not of the external world itself, but of our particular impression of it, the "involuntary sensations" that might come from it.

The artist is studying the laws of man and nature. His experiments and discoveries are "as delicate as those of science," and he must be as faithful to these truths as is the scientist. What causal law is (or was) to the scientist, the metaphor is to the artist. In searching for order, unity, and laws, the scientist must also create as much as discover them. Seeing order in nature, and expressing it in a work of art as Proust had done, reveals the same activity as that of a scientist. Seeing the line and circle suggested by the bottom and top of the madeleine as a reflection of the linear and circular structure of the novel, itself manifesting a view of the world, is no different than astronomer Johannes Kepler's search for unity in all of nature, or physicists Ernest Rutherford and Niels Bohr finding a model for the atom in the planetary system. The scientist and the artist share a fundamental belief in a harmonious universe that will reveal itself in underlying symmetrical patterns. That Kepler's research in the 16th and 17th centuries into the movement of the planets was based on a belief in the music of the spheres is not as bizarre or "unscientific" as it might at first seem. The same may be said for Proust's quest for the essence of the self and the world in such illogical, disparate activities as tasting a madeleine, hearing a piece of music, smelling the varnish of a stairway, seeing some steeples, or tripping over paving stones. His vision, reaching, as it does, from the smallest, most microscopic detail, to the largest, most cosmic perception, reflects a similar comprehensive view on the part of the modern physicist, where particle physics is united with the study of the universe.

However, have we not drifted from the discussion of psychology to that of cosmologies? Not at all, for our vision of the world has as much to do with our vision of ourselves as it does with the world external to us. What lies outside of us are facts, and the meaning comes from an individual's creative mind, like a projection from the magic lantern onto an already existing wall. The psychologist, the artist, and the physicist, all share a belief in the fundamental interrelatedness of nature, and a dedication to truth. While it may be argued that the artist's emphasis is on a reflection of inner, subjective truth, whereas the scientist's is on external, "objective" reality, their activities are indeed fundamentally interwoven.

When Proust wrote of finding the essence of both things and self in the privileged moments where his "special pleasure" united the essence of sensations from the past and present, taking him out of the contingencies of time and space, intelligence only played an *a posteriori* role to intuition's *a priori* status. Man's unconscious is the connecting wire, the means of communication between these two essences.

"The fusion of subject and object"

It is here, then, in this relegated status of intelligence, will, and reason that the fusion of subject and object, that the essence of both man and the things is found. This change reflects that of the philosophy of the German romantics in general and Friedrich Schelling in particular. The participation of the unconscious in an underlying reality which unites the essence of both self and world finds its source in Schopenhauer's theory of an *Ungrund*–the abyss of eternity–and of a world as infinite Will. Speaking generally, the German romantics perceived here a philosophy of art, uniting self and world in a vitalistic yet quasi-scientific way. This intersubjective unity is clearly evident in Proust's novel, when the Narrator describes the artist as belonging to a sort of international, unknown country. This German romanticism also affected Carl Jung and was likely the origin of the similarities evident in his theory of archetypes and synchronicity, as well as Proust's aesthetic theories.

   A chance encounter with some apparently insignificant object, devoid of any intellectual interest, serving both to unite subject and object and to form the basis for involuntary memory, aroused an involuntary sensation in Proust. By uniting past and present, this involuntary memory permits an escape from the contingencies of time and space and, through its instinctive expression in a work of art, the essence of both self and world manifests itself. The result of this process is a certainty, an acausal connecting principle, which is at the same time found and created.

Jung's theory of synchronicity

At the beginning of "Synchronicity: An Acausal Connection Principle," Jung referred to Schopenhauer as an influence on ideas such as those of the simultaneity of the causally unconnected, or "chance." In his theory of synchronicity, Jung looked at "coincidental" events and tried to organize them into "meaningful dispersions," contrasting them with simply random events. Statistical analysis, of course, participates in a similar activity, but Jung's methodology differed in its use of psychological archetypes as a basis of organization. He defined synchronicity as a "psychically conditioned relativity of space and time." Neither will, nor intelligence, nor reason is relevant to the search, as we saw in each of the Proustian encounters leading to an experience of the "special pleasure." There must be a state of consciousness similar to Janet's "lowering of the mental level," that is to say, "a certain narrowing of consciousness and a corresponding strengthening of the unconscious." This state of mind serves to allow not only the unconscious, archetypal truths to emerge from the human psyche, but it also permits the corresponding underlying forms in nature to reveal themselves, undisturbed by any rationally ordered projection onto it. Whereas the mechanistic scientific attitude assumes a unity between reason and intelligence in man's consciousness and a causal order in nature, the Jungian theory of synchronicity compels one to assume that there is already something that exists in man's consciousness that has no causal reason for existing. These two worldviews are not mutually exclusive. Both assume a possible unity and can co-exist, one on the level of "objective" or causal connections, and the other on a "subjective," or "coincidental" plane of interconnections. For a number of reasons, this theory cannot be proven according to the requirement of causal verification, one of the criteria of mechanistic science. This, too, is the case with modern physics, both on the smallest scale, in quantum physics, and in the largest dimension, where relativity reigns. What we must do is look at the meaningful groupings, at the archetypes, and consider both their essential simplicity, and their universal applicability (two other basic requirements of any law) in all fields where the human psyche and nature come together: in science, in religion, and in art. According to Jung, an archetype constitutes the structure of the collective unconscious. As with Proust's "special pleasure," it is both invented and discovered.

In the design metaphorically drawn by the experience with the steeples of Martinville and Vieuxvicq, we see the movement from the line (suggested by the steeples) to the circle (as drawn by the motion of the steeples). Several fundamental themes which concerned Proust are described in the novel: time, space, and the unconscious. The image can be seen in every field of man's effort to describe himself and his world: in science, in religion, and in art.

At the top of the circle, with the steeple (or the "finger of God") pointed upwards, towards the infinite of the sky, we also see associated themes of light, the day and, as we shall see at the end of the description of the movements described here, creation. In daylight, the steeples are described as three birds and as three flowers after sundown. The three steeples also make the Narrator think of "three young girls in a legend, abandoned in a solitude where obscurity was already falling." The introduction of the three girls can be seen as a suggestion of the sensual aspects of the sensorial experience which, for the artist, can lead into the depths of the unconscious.

In the diagram, the steeples can be seen to metaphorically fall first to a horizontal position, reflecting a contact with the finite world, the world known through perception and the senses. The Narrator has encountered no God, he has a sensorial experience of an object on the same plane. Then, with the experience of the 'special pleasure' there is an inversion, a movement toward the "landscape of the self."

The unconscious is associated with night and, in war-time Paris, the Narrator can be said to have reached the depths of darkness in this apocalyptic scene. While Charlus has gone "to the end" of his essential nature and, in a sense, will never find any pleasure beyond that found chez Jupien, the artist will escape the confines of the darkness of the night and of the unconscious. The movement shown in the diagram will continue. The artist will project the essence of the unconscious found in the inverted voyage into the self onto his work of art. Like a magic lantern shining onto a screen or a wall, he will project his discoveries onto the blank canvas, or the white page, or whatever the medium may be, and create.

At the end of *Time Regained*, the Narrator completes the movement of the diagram, metaphorically bringing the steeple back up to the light of creation, in "the most beautiful day" at the Guermantes' home. The God is now the artist. He has created the word, the work of art. His pleasure is not like Charlus's; it is found in the experience of his involuntary memory. As such, it is not chained to the contingencies of the causal order of time and space. Without the voyage into the darkness of the self, the creative act would not be possible. It is in this sense that one does not only look, but one creates, and vice versa. Inside of each person is a book of signs, and the artist's work is similar to that of a translator. The laws manifested in this translation have nothing to do with either the mechanistic rules of classical science or those of religious morality, or of critical rules. They are created in solitude, according to their own truths.

While the theory of archetypes cannot be proved, it is hoped that this brief effort to probe into the background of one of these "signs" in Proust's novel will suggest the richness of their archetypal value. In the union of subject and object, of psyche and world, they suggest an acausal connecting principle, an order, a certainty which has dominated man's vision of the world and himself. Their recreation in Proust's novel suggests not only a certainty based on the instinctive creation of one man's involuntary memory; they also reflect a certainty, an essential connection which unites the unconscious order in the psyche of the human race with a symmetry in the surrounding universe

The search for a comprehensive worldview

Critics have approached the novel from various scientific viewpoints: optical, botanical, physical, and psychological. The influences that various scientific disciplines had on Proust are apparent on every level of the novel and provide both a historical and a philosophical perspective from which to view it.

While art and science have separate methods of inquiry and expression, both encounter the limits inherent in the gathering of supposed "objective" knowledge. They grow out of a shared need to find (or create) order in an otherwise chaotic universe. This chapter is arranged in such a way as to show how Proust's novel reflects this search for a comprehensive worldview. It concludes with a hypothesis whose purpose is to suggest particular archetypal evidence of the end result of this search. We have seen how Proust's references to glass and optics reflect "modern" developments in industry, art, medicine, and theoretical science. They provide a terminology that allowed him to express his theories on art, time, man, and world in a "scientific" manner. They also show the basic fallacy of the positivistic outlook. While providing new means to probe the nature of man and world, they ultimately show that no certainty can be derived from a knowledge whose very foundation (the objective perception of the world ruled by laws based on fixed references in time and space, and which can be communicated intellectually and without distortion) is in question.

The repeated failure of the positivistic world view to provide any solid ground for certainty leads the search outward, from the Narrator's room to the stars. At each stage in this voyage, the narrator encounters the limits in both the Cartesian conception of man and the Newtonian notion of nature.

Motion, change, novelty: all are essential to the formation of Proust's "immense edifice of memory"—his novel. Each "special pleasure," experienced in a non-willed, sensory contact with something external to him (the magic lantern, the varnish on the stairway, the madeleine, the steeples, etc.), provides him with an involuntary memory. In contrast with a positivistic methodology, involuntary memory provides a kind of knowledge that is not based on a questionable, albeit rational, objective subject observing a phenomenon whose causal laws are equally in question. Each experience in this movement that leads the Narrator outward, into the world external to himself, paradoxically forces the Narrator back into himself. The essence of the experience is found in the subject, not in the object.

We saw the search turn inward, toward the observing subject–man. What is his essence? How can it be found? How can it be expressed? The essence lies in the "special pleasure" experienced in a sensory contact with an external object. Unlike an experiment performed according to positivist methodology, it cannot be willed or caused to happen. It can only be brought about by a chance encounter. It is not the product of rational analysis, but of intuitive creation. Its expression is not in an intellectual treatise; it is in a metaphor.

Therefore, while we have seen evidence of a classical–or positivistic–search in Proust's novel, the Narrator is ultimately forced to create a new methodology, a "modern" worldview. His predicament reflects that of the newly emerging form of inquiry known as psychology. How, the psychologists also asked, can one arrive at the essence of the self? How can one observe the "real" self of man, his unconscious, without any conscious distortions? As we have seen, what free association was for Freud, involuntary memory was for Proust. Both provide information that is not dependent on any rational, conscious participation on the part of either the observer or the observed. Here, subject and object, observer and observed, man and world are united. For Proust, the contingencies of time and space are replaced by an acausal, atemporal principle. The essence of both man and world is distilled, fixed, and expressed in a metaphor. What causal law is to science, the metaphor is to art and, while the latter cannot, of course, be said to replace the former in the real world, it may be seen as its complement. While Proust's extensive use of metaphor does appear to stand in lieu of scientific certainty and references to laws are found throughout his novel, the Narrator's artistic creation is meant, rather as a homology.

The diagram suggested by the steeples of Martinville and Vieuxvicq is not presented as archetypal proof (if indeed such proof may be possible). It is an efficient means to summarize what happens in the experience of the 'special pleasure,' to organize a discussion on the novel's structure, and to begin a discussion of archetypal undercurrents in the novel.

11. The Reader: Riding the Proust Wave

The Narrator's story is the search for a vocation. In his case, this means being a writer, in particular a novelist. He takes the reader along on the sometimes tortuous, lonely, and uncertain path one must take to get there. For Richard Bales, "This surely is Proust's greatest contribution to literature, that he manages to make each reader identify so closely with his Narrator as to seem to participate in the creative act itself." He is certainly a writer's writer but, as seen on the first page of *In Search of Lost Time*, his role as a reader is also essential, as it was in Proust's life. The dissolving of the boundary between book and reader as the older Narrator falls asleep while reading, also happens to the Narrator as a child, but without the transitional aid of falling asleep in the process. The Narrator's grandmother admonishes him to go outside so, not wanting any further interruption in his reading, he goes to read under a chestnut tree in the garden. Here, the world around him dissolves, as his consciousness "would simultaneously unfold while [he] was reading, and which ranged from the most deeply hidden aspirations of [his] being to the wholly external view of the horizon...." Internally, he is taken to his "innermost impulse, the lever whose incessant movements controlled everything else, [his] belief in the philosophic richness and beauty of the book [he] was reading." The novelist can help by substituting the opaqueness of what Françoise, aunt Léonie's maid, calls "real people" with "their equivalent in immaterial sections, things, that is, that the soul can assimilate." Once assimilated, it is in the reader that the novel's events are occurring as they might in a dream, "but a dream more lucid and more abiding than those which come to us in sleep."

There have been many comparisons between Proust and his contemporary, Sigmund Freud, who is said to have "discovered" the unconscious. The Narrator's quest makes him a frequent traveler down what Freud called in his *Interpretation of Dreams* "the royal road to a knowledge of the unconscious." He relishes the ride and often describes those fluid moments during which sleep provides the transition between the conscious and the unconscious self. One of the most commonly applied Freudian approaches uses his notion of infantile sexuality and the Oedipus complex. In short, the Narrator's childhood need for his mother's goodnight kiss—and its refusal—explains his later, obsessively jealous love for Albertine: "Unfortunately ... the kiss that Albertine would give me when she left me for the night, very different from her usual kiss, would no more soothe me than my mother's kiss had soothed me long ago, on days when she was vexed with me." The effects of the demystification of the Romantic notion of love cannot be overestimated. Love is no longer a metaphysical ideal, but a natural phenomenon. The psychologist and the artist now have a "scientific" tool they can use, an "objective" perspective from which they can study the manifestations of sexual desire and a terminology with which they can theorize about and express its nature and its origin. However, while it is true that the Narrator's love for Albertine reveals the Proustian unconscious, to stop here, at an unconscious based on a libidinous, oedipal force manifesting itself as sexual appetite, would place a superficial limitation not only on the Proustian, but also on the Freudian concept of the unconscious. For Freud, the unconscious was also apparent in the ego and the superego. According to the British scholar Malcolm Bowie, Proust thought the unconscious was "so enlarged and so copious as to make the Freudian unconscious seem a miserably stunted affair." Proust's thirst for knowledge was more insatiable than any simple sexual appetite. If it can be said that Freud "discovered" the unconscious, then it can also be posited that Proust "created" it in *In Search of Lost Time*.

    Freud and Proust shared the belief that the unconscious is repressed and both described the unconscious topographically as being located beneath the social, conscious self. The Narrator is constantly searching for those revealing moments in human conduct, for any cracks in the conscious constructs that might reveal the hidden unconscious. Like a psychologist, the Narrator observes "Freudian slips" wherever and whenever he can. These observations are, in fact, an essential part of his vocation as an artist: "The stupidest people, in their gestures, their remarks, the sentiments which they involuntarily express, manifest laws which they do not themselves perceive but which the artist surprises in them." But should one stop here, accepting the Narrator's theories and his own self-analysis as accurate, even though the observations come from a subject who is aware of being observed and whose actions are being recorded? Can the Narrator's hypothesizing, based on his many observations of other people's actions, be trusted? Or, like the Narrator, must the reader also look behind any conscious, rational explanations for hidden, unconscious motives and, if so, how? In order to get a true picture of the unconscious in Proust's novel, one must first allow it to reveal itself through images, words, and any apparently insignificant detail that makes itself known through some unconscious reaction.

Reading can inform us about many things, but the most important lesson is what the reader learns about his or her own self in the process. It is as royal a road to the unconscious as the analysis of dreams was to Freud. Auto-analysis, the examination of one's self, was not possible for either Freud or Proust. *In Search of Lost Time* is a sort of magical mirror that, when stepped into, can reveal the inner self of each reader. Or perhaps it is something more scientific: "In reality every reader is, while he is reading, the reader of his own self. The writer's work is merely a kind of optical instrument which he offers to the reader to enable him to discern what, without the book, he would perhaps never have perceived in himself."

Objectivity versus subjectivity

To be truly objective, anyone looking for historical or biographical knowledge is placed outside the author, in their actions, communications, notes, publications, etc. But what do you do if the knowledge of the self takes place on the inside, and, furthermore, must be of a subjective nature, not susceptible to being known by positivistic methods and objectives? The only way the unconscious self can be known is in a subjective manner, taking place "inside" the reader and not determined by the author. One can look at historical facts and descriptions to see the ways Proust became aware of and experienced the self and the unconscious, like the case of Félida in *La Revue scientifique* by Dr. Charles Azam in 1876. The observations of the woman led to a new paradigm. There was a division in the self that made the existence of at least one other self, the unconscious, undeniable. The division between the conscious and the unconscious, between voluntary memory and involuntary memory, between the social self and the creative self, was made possible by this case. The research into the treatments that Proust underwent, from 1905 to 1906 with the French psychologist Dr. Paul Sollier, is also important, as different ideas surrounding developments in psychology that were circulating at the time made several personal descriptions by individuals who were with Proust during one of his spiritual/phenomenological/transcendental experiences possible. The best known of these is the one already discussed, when Reynaldo Hahn described Proust standing transfixed and unmoving among the Bengal roses. This event incited numerous critical comments—for example, that Proust was "sucking the objects through his eyes," and "let himself be seduced by the essence of the roses."

Despite the different degrees of importance given to the look and to the object, there is the same fundamental relationship between subject and object: between Proust, the person observing and the roses, the objects being observed. What is clear is that any knowledge of the self depends not only on an isolated self, of a subject without an object. The Cartesian self that only depends on a thinking self is decentralized, pulled toward the world outside itself. Proust, like his Narrator, must look outside in order to see inside. But the filters through which all of this is known must also be considered. Does Hahn's perspective not play a role? And is his memory not subjected to the same limits as our own? And who knows if having another person present with him did not influence the event for Proust? And is the self known through these descriptions? Can it be known from external sources? The knowledge gained by Proust about his unconscious took place internally, in his self. Historical and biographical knowledge can only see its manifestations externally.

But how does one penetrate the external to arrive at the internal Proust? Can one pierce the plurality of selves to arrive at a profound and essential self? One can look at the projections of the magic lantern of his self onto the screen of his novel: "Through art alone are we able to emerge from ourselves, to know what another person sees, of a universe which is not the same as our own and of which, without art, the landscapes would remain as unknown to us as those that may exist on the moon." Perhaps the "special radiance" of *In Search of Lost Time* can shed light on the means by which Proust traveled through the darkness of his unconscious. As we have seen, it is in the experience of a "special pleasure," one of those privileged moments when the extra-temporal joy is experienced from "the obscure countryside of my self." Dreams are also, as they were for Freud, "royal roads" to the unconscious. Depending on the expertise of the writer and the receptivity of the reader, a book becomes another means of exploration into the unconscious, both in the book and the reader. And if Proust used his experiences with his own unconscious to create his "series of novels of the Unconscious," perhaps it also provided the means of knowing his own unconscious. And whose unconscious would he have explored if not his own? In the right hands, is the right novel (especially one that is "a series of novels of the Unconscious"), a sort of conducting wire of the unconscious, the waves passing through from author, to text to reader?

Schopenhauer's theories also influenced Jung and are the origin of some of the parallels that can be seen between his theories of archetypes and synchronicity and those we have discussed here regarding Proust. With the scientist Wolfgang Pauli, Jung published the *Interpretation of Nature and the Psyche*. For the first time in known history, two specialists—one from the internal world of psychology and the other from the external world of physics – got together to describe a unified vision of the essences of man and world. In the beginning of his part of the book, "Synchronicity: An A-Causal Connecting Principle," Jung referred to Schopenhauer. As with Proust, coincidence replaced causality, and he organized events that happened by chance into significant constellations in contrast to events that are simply without a cause of any sort. Statistical analysis plays a role, but Jung's methodology is based on his use of psychological archetypes as an organizing principle. As with Proust, there is a "lowering of the mental level, that is, a certain diminution of the conscious mind and a growth of the unconscious." This mental state allows not only unconscious truths and archetypes to appear in the human psyche, but also lets corresponding forms in nature reveal themselves without being disturbed by reason. Where positivistic science presumes a unity between reason and intelligence in man and a causal order in nature, the Jungian theory of synchronicity presumes that there is "in the unconscious something like an *a priori* knowledge ... that lacks any fundamental causality." These two worldviews do not exclude each other. The mistake would be to accept solely positivistic and causal knowledge of the world and man that is governed only by Newtonian and Cartesian laws. With the theory of synchronicity, there is a methodology and a terminology that help to understand the unconscious in *In Search of Lost Time*.

Proust and hypnotism

According to Jung, archetypes "constitute the structure of the collective unconscious." He made a comment similar to that of the Narrator after he tastes the madeleine and herbal tea and says, "Seek? More than that, to create." When he continued his description of archetypes as ideal, *a priori* forms that are as much found as invented, Jung remarked that "they are *discovered* in that one was not conscious of their unconscious and autonomous existence and *invented* in the sense that their presence was inferred by analogous conceptual structures."

In each person, there is a book of signs. According to Proust, the work of a writer is that of a translator: "… the only true book … does not have to be 'invented' by a great writer–for it exists already in each of us–[it] has to be translated by him. The function and the task of a writer are those of a translator." The laws manifested in this translation have nothing to do with either the mechanistic rules of classical science or with any religious morality or critical or political "correctness." They are created in solitude, according to their own truths: "As for the inner book of unknown symbols (symbols carved in relief they might have been, which my attention, as it explored my unconscious, groped for and stumbled against and followed the contours of, like a diver exploring the ocean bed), if I tried to read them no one could help me with any rules, for to read them was an act of creation in which no one can do our work for us or even collaborate with us."

With Proust, there was a "re-centralization" of the identity of the novel, from that which was placed between the author and the text, to that situated between the reader and the text. For the Proust scholar Antoine Compagnon, it is there that the unity of the text is realized. It is clear that Proust made every effort to reach out and engage the reader, to include him or her in the Narrator's quest, blurring the boundaries between his novel and the reader, preparing the terrain as well as possible for a fortuitous encounter between the unconscious of the book and that of the reader.

In his *Introduction to Psychology*, Freud referred to hypnotism as the means by which the unconscious made itself apparent. Perhaps it can also provide another road to the unconscious or, at least, facilitate the trip? Adrien Proust's experiences with Emile X and Marcel's own experiences with Dr. Sollier make it clear that the novelist was keenly aware of this trance-like state. Despite his apparent disappointment with his treatments and no knowledge of exactly what went on during his sessions with Dr. Sollier, hypnotism must have appealed to Proust as a means of providing the desired lowering of the conscious self and opening the individual to suggestion. It should not come as a surprise that he would try to employ such means of preparing the reader to fall into the world of his novel. Given his use of modern developments in psychology and other fields, it would be surprising if he did not use it. Look at the first pages of the novel that Bowie called "a three-thousand page incantation." They are about falling asleep, losing the confines of identity, time, and space, and becoming part of the book. What might seem boring to some is Proust preparing the reader by creating a state of receptivity to suggestion, setting the stage for a long, extraordinary experience.

What matters is what happens when (and if) you, the reader, experience the voyage of discovery in *In Search of Lost Time* and, if you experience coincidences between the novel and your own life, do not be alarmed. It is just Proust's hypnotic magic.

Sources

William C. Carter's *Marcel Proust: A Life* was a constant resource while writing this book. It is by far the most substantive and trustworthy biography written. If you would like a well-written, more detailed description of the genesis of the novel and Proust's own life and times, you should read Carter's book.

Translations from French to English are taken from the Modern Library edition of *In Search of Lost Time* (translators C. K. Scott Moncrieff and Andreas Mayor) or are my own.

Suggested Reading

In English

The choice of which edition of *In Search of Lost Time* to read in English depends on what you want from it. If you would like an excellent abridged edition of Proust's novel that is informative without being intrusive, William C. Carter's version, published by Yale Press, is the best you can read. If you want to read the text alone, the Modern Library translation is probably the best and most readily available edition.

Céleste Albaret, *Monsieur Proust*. Trans. Barbara Bray. New York: New York Review of Books Classics, 2003.

Patrick Alexander, *Marcel Proust's Search for Lost Time: A Reader's Guide to "The Remembrance of Things Past"*. New York: Vintage Books, 2007.

Richard Bales, *A la recherche du temps perdu*. London: Grant & Cutler Ltd., 1995.

--, ed. *The Cambridge Companion to Proust*. Cambridge: Cambridge University Press, 2001.

Samuel Beckett, *Proust*. New York: Grove Press, 1931.

Malcolm Bowie, *Proust Among the Stars*. New York: Columbia University Press, 1998.

--, *Freud, Proust and Lacan: Theory as Fiction*. Cambridge: Cambridge University Press, 1987.

William Carter, *Marcel Proust: A Life*. New Haven: Yale University Press, 2000.

--, ed. and ann. *In Search of Lost Time*. New Haven: Yale University Press. Seven volumes. Volume 1, 2013, Volume 2, 2015.

Stéphane Heuet, "*In Search of Lost Time*": "*Swann's Way*": *A Graphic Novel*. Trans. Arthur Goldhammer. New York: Liveright, 2015.

Jack Jordan, *Marcel Proust's "A la recherche du temps perdu"*: *A Search for Certainty*. Birmingham: Summa Publications, 1993.
Eric Karpeles, *Paintings in Proust*. London: Thames & Hudson, 2008.
Roger Shattuck, *Proust's Binoculars*. New York: Random House, 1963.
--, *Marcel Proust*. New York: The Viking Press, 1974.

In French

There are several editions of *À la recherche du temps perdu* in French, but it comes down to two quite different choices. The first is the Folio edition in paperback. It is the cheaper of the two choices by far and is a sturdy basic text, the one used by most people. The second is the beautiful but expensive four-volume, leather-bound, and well-annotated Pléiade version edited by Jean-Yves Tadié. Both are from the publisher, Gallimard.

Jean-Louis Baudry, *Proust, Freud et l'autre*. Paris: Les Editions de Minuit, 1984.
Edward Bizub, *Proust et le moi divisé*. Genève: Librairie Droz, 2006.
Annick Bouillaguet et Brian G. Rogers, *Dictionnaire Marcel Proust*. Paris: Champion Classiques, 2014.
Elisabeth Czoniczer, *Quelques antécédents de "A la recherche du temps perdu": tendances qui peuvent avoir contribué à la cristallisation du roman proustien*. Genève: Librairie Droz, 1957.
Antoine Galland, trans., *Les Mille et Une nuits*. 3 vols. Paris: Garnier Flammarion, 1965.
Anne Henry, *Marcel Proust: théories pour une esthétique*. Paris: Klincksieck, 1981.
Philip Kolb, *Marcel Proust: Correspondance*. 21 vols. Paris: Plon, 1971-1993.

André Maurois, *A la recherche de Marcel Proust*. Paris: Hachette, 1949.

Paul Morand, *Le visiteur du soir*. Genève: La Palatine, 1949.

Claude Pichois, *Vitesse et vision du monde*. Neuchatel: Editions de la Baconnière, 1973.

Marcel Plantevignes, *Avec Marcel Proust: causeries-souvenirs sur Cabourg et le boulevard Haussmann*. Paris: Nizet, 1966.

Georges Poulet, *L'Espace proustien*. Paris: Gallimard, 1963.

Jacques Rivière, *Quelques progrès dans l'étude du coeur humain (Freud et Proust)*. Paris: Librairie de France, 1926.

Jean-Yves Tadié, *Proust*. Paris: Pierre Belfond, 1983.

Camille Vettard, *Marcel Proust: Lettres inédites*. Bagnères-de-Bigorre: Maurice Péré, 1926.